DENTAL HEALTH

GENERAL EDITORS

Dale C. Garell, M.D.
Medical Director, California Children Services, Department of Health Services, County of Los Angeles
Associate Dean for Curriculum; Clinical Professor, Department of Pediatrics & Family Medicine, University of Southern California School of Medicine
Former President, Society for Adolescent Medicine

Solomon H. Snyder, M.D.
Distinguished Service Professor of Neuroscience, Pharmacology, and Psychiatry, Johns Hopkins University School of Medicine
Former President, Society for Neuroscience
Albert Lasker Award in Medical Research, 1978

CONSULTING EDITORS

Robert W. Blum, M.D., Ph.D.
Professor and Director, Division of General Pediatrics and Adolescent Health, University of Minnesota

Charles E. Irwin, Jr., M.D.
Professor of Pediatrics; Director, Division of Adolescent Medicine, University of California, San Francisco

Lloyd J. Kolbe, Ph.D.
Director of the Division of Adolescent and School Health, Center for Chronic Disease Prevention and Health Promotion, Centers for Disease Control

Jordan J. Popkin
Former Director, Division of Federal Employee Occupational Health, U.S. Public Health Service Region I

Joseph L. Rauh, M.D.
Professor of Pediatrics and Medicine, Adolescent Medicine, Children's Hospital Medical Center, Cincinnati
Former President, Society for Adolescent Medicine

THE ENCYCLOPEDIA OF
H E A L T H

THE HEALTHY BODY

Dale C. Garell, M.D. · General Editor

DISCARD

DENTAL HEALTH

Dorothy Siegel

Introduction by C. Everett Koop, M.D., Sc.D.
former Surgeon General, U. S. Public Health Service

CHELSEA HOUSE PUBLISHERS

New York · Philadelphia

The goal of the ENCYCLOPEDIA OF HEALTH *is to provide general information in the ever-changing areas of physiology, psychology, and related medical issues. The titles in this series are not intended to take the place of the professional advice of a physician or other health care professional.*

CHELSEA HOUSE PUBLISHERS
EDITORIAL DIRECTOR   Richard Rennert
EXECUTIVE MANAGING EDITOR   Karyn Gullen Browne
EXECUTIVE EDITOR   Sean Dolan
COPY CHIEF   Robin James
PICTURE EDITOR   Adrian G. Allen
ART DIRECTOR   Robert Mitchell
MANUFACTURING DIRECTOR   Gerald Levine
PRODUCTION COORDINATOR   Marie Claire Cebrián-Ume

The Encyclopedia of Health
SENIOR EDITOR   Don Nardo

Staff for DENTAL HEALTH
EDITORIAL ASSISTANT   Mary B. Sisson
PICTURE RESEARCHER   Sandy Jones
DESIGNER   M. Cambraia Magalhães

Library of Congress Cataloging-in-Publication Data

Siegel, Dorothy.
    Dental Health/Dorothy Siegel
        p. cm.—(The Encyclopedia of health)
    Includes bibliographical references and index.
    Summary: Discusses how teeth and jaws function, their diseases, and strategies for maintaining good dental health.
    ISBN 0-7910-0014-1
        0-7910-0454-6 (pbk.)
    1. Dental care—Juvenile literature. 2. Dentistry—Juvenile literature. 3. Teeth—Juvenile literature. [1. Dental care. 2. Dentistry. 3. Teeth.] I. Title. II. Series.
RK63.S53 1993   92-45205
617.6'01—dc20   CIP
                                                                           AC

CONTENTS

"Prevention and Education:
The Keys to Good Health"—
C. Everett Koop, M.D., Sc.D.   7

Foreword—Dale C. Garell, M.D.   11

1   The Teeth   13

2   How the Teeth and Jaws Function   25

3   Dental Problems   35

4   Basic Dental Therapy   45

5   Gum Diseases   61

6   Taking Care of the Teeth   69

7   Orthodontics   81

8   Looking Ahead   91

Appendix: For More Information   101

Further Reading   102

Glossary   104

Index   107

THE ENCYCLOPEDIA OF
H E A L T H

THE HEALTHY BODY

The Circulatory System
Dental Health
The Digestive System
The Endocrine System
Exercise
Genetics & Heredity
The Human Body: An Overview
Hygiene
The Immune System
Memory & Learning
The Musculoskeletal System
The Nervous System
Nutrition
The Reproductive System
The Respiratory System
The Senses
Sleep
Speech & Hearing
Sports Medicine
Vision
Vitamins & Minerals

THE LIFE CYCLE

Adolescence
Adulthood
Aging
Childhood
Death & Dying
The Family
Friendship & Love
Pregnancy & Birth

MEDICAL ISSUES

Careers in Health Care
Environmental Health
Folk Medicine
Health Care Delivery
Holistic Medicine
Medical Ethics
Medical Fakes & Frauds
Medical Technology
Medicine & the Law
Occupational Health
Public Health

PSYCHOLOGICAL DISORDERS AND THEIR TREATMENT

Anxiety & Phobias
Child Abuse
Compulsive Behavior
Delinquency & Criminal Behavior
Depression
Diagnosing & Treating Mental Illness
Eating Habits & Disorders
Learning Disabilities
Mental Retardation
Personality Disorders
Schizophrenia
Stress Management
Suicide

MEDICAL DISORDERS AND THEIR TREATMENT

AIDS
Allergies
Alzheimer's Disease
Arthritis
Birth Defects
Cancer
The Common Cold
Diabetes
Emergency Medicine
Gynecological Disorders
Headaches
The Hospital
Kidney Disorders
Medical Diagnosis
The Mind-Body Connection
Mononucleosis and Other Infectious Diseases
Nuclear Medicine
Organ Transplants
Pain
Physical Handicaps
Poisons & Toxins
Prescription & OTC Drugs
Sexually Transmitted Diseases
Skin Disorders
Stroke & Heart Disease
Substance Abuse
Tropical Medicine

PREVENTION AND EDUCATION: THE KEYS TO GOOD HEALTH

C. Everett Koop, M.D., Sc.D.
former Surgeon General,
U.S. Public Health Service

The issue of health education has received particular attention in recent years because of the presence of AIDS in the news. But our response to this particular tragedy points up a number of broader issues that doctors, public health officials, educators, and the public face. In particular, it points up the necessity for sound health education for citizens of all ages.

Over the past 25 years this country has been able to bring about dramatic declines in the death rates for heart disease, stroke, accidents, and for people under the age of 45, cancer. Today, Americans generally eat better and take better care of themselves than ever before. Thus, with the help of modern science and technology, they have a better chance of surviving serious—even catastrophic—illnesses. That's the good news.

But, like every phonograph record, there's a flip side, and one with special significance for young adults. According to a report issued in 1979 by Dr. Julius Richmond, my predecessor as Surgeon General, Americans aged 15 to 24 had a higher death rate in 1979 than they did 20 years earlier. The causes: violent death and injury, alcohol and drug abuse, unwanted pregnancies, and sexually transmitted diseases. Adolescents are particularly vulnerable because they are beginning to explore their own sexuality and perhaps to experiment with drugs. The need for educating young people is critical, and the price of neglect is high.

Yet even for the population as a whole, our health is still far from what it could be. Why? A 1974 Canadian government report attributed all death and disease to four broad elements: inadequacies in the health care system, behavioral factors or unhealthy life-styles, environmental hazards, and human biological factors.

To be sure, there are diseases that are still beyond the control of even our advanced medical knowledge and techniques. And despite yearnings that are as old as the human race itself, there is no "fountain of youth" to ward off aging and death. Still, there is a solution to many of the problems that undermine sound health. In a word, that solution is prevention. Prevention, which includes health promotion and education, saves lives, improves the quality of life, and in the long run, saves money.

In the United States, organized public health activities and preventive medicine have a long history. Important milestones in this country or foreign breakthroughs adopted in the United States include the improvement of sanitary procedures and the development of pasteurized milk in the late 19th century and the introduction in the mid-20th century of effective vaccines against polio, measles, German measles, mumps, and other once-rampant diseases. Internationally, organized public health efforts began on a wide-scale basis with the International Sanitary Conference of 1851, to which 12 nations sent representatives. The World Health Organization, founded in 1948, continues these efforts under the aegis of the United Nations, with particular emphasis on combating communicable diseases and the training of health care workers.

Despite these accomplishments, much remains to be done in the field of prevention. For too long, we have had a medical care system that is science- and technology-based, focused, essentially, on illness and mortality. It is now patently obvious that both the social and the economic costs of such a system are becoming insupportable.

Implementing prevention—and its corollaries, health education and promotion—is the job of several groups of people.

First, the medical and scientific professions need to continue basic scientific research, and here we are making considerable progress. But increased concern with prevention will also have a decided impact on how primary care doctors practice medicine. With a shift to health-based rather than morbidity-based medicine, the role of the "new physician" will include a healthy dose of patient education.

Second, practitioners of the social and behavioral sciences—psychologists, economists, city planners—along with lawyers, business leaders, and government officials—must solve the practical and ethical dilemmas confronting us: poverty, crime, civil rights, literacy, education, employment, housing, sanitation, environmental protection, health care delivery systems, and so forth. All of these issues affect public health.

Third is the public at large. We'll consider that very important group in a moment.

Fourth, and the linchpin in this effort, is the public health profession—doctors, epidemiologists, teachers—who must harness the professional expertise of the first two groups and the common sense and cooperation of the third, the public. They must define the problems statistically and qualitatively and then help us set priorities for finding the solutions.

To a very large extent, improving those statistics is the responsibility of every individual. So let's consider more specifically what the role of the individual should be and why health education is so important to that role. First, and most obvious, individuals can protect themselves from illness and injury and thus minimize their need for professional medical care. They can eat nutritious food; get adequate exercise; avoid tobacco, alcohol, and drugs; and take prudent steps to avoid accidents. The proverbial "apple a day keeps the doctor away" is not so far from the truth, after all.

Second, individuals should actively participate in their own medical care. They should schedule regular medical and dental checkups. Should they develop an illness or injury, they should know when to treat themselves and when to seek professional help. To gain the maximum benefit from any medical treatment that they do require, individuals must become partners in that treatment. For instance, they should understand the effects and side effects of medications. I counsel young physicians that there is no such thing as too much information when talking with patients. But the corollary is the patient must know enough about the nuts and bolts of the healing process to understand what the doctor is telling him or her. That is at least partially the patient's responsibility.

Education is equally necessary for us to understand the ethical and public policy issues in health care today. Sometimes individuals will encounter these issues in making decisions about their own treatment or that of family members. Other citizens may encounter them as jurors in medical malpractice cases. But we all become involved, indirectly, when we elect our public officials, from school board members to the president. Should surrogate parenting be legal? To what extent is drug testing desirable, legal, or necessary? Should there be public funding for family planning, hospitals, various types of medical research, and other medical care for the indigent? How should we allocate scant technological resources, such as kidney dialysis and organ transplants? What is the proper role of government in protecting the rights of patients?

What are the broad goals of public health in the United States today? In 1980, the Public Health Service issued a report aptly entitled *Promoting Health—Preventing Disease: Objectives for the Nation*. This report expressed its goals in terms of mortality and in terms of intermediate goals in education and health improvement. It identified 15 major concerns: controlling high blood pressure; improving family planning; improving pregnancy care and infant health; increasing the rate of immunization; controlling sexually transmitted diseases; controlling the presence of toxic agents and radiation in the environment; improving occupational safety and health; preventing accidents; promoting water fluoridation and dental health; controlling infectious diseases; decreasing smoking; decreasing alcohol and drug abuse; improving nutrition; promoting physical fitness and exercise; and controlling stress and violent behavior.

For healthy adolescents and young adults (ages 15 to 24), the specific goal was a 20% reduction in deaths, with a special focus on motor vehicle injuries and alcohol and drug abuse. For adults (ages 25 to 64), the aim was 25% fewer deaths, with a concentration on heart attacks, strokes, and cancers.

Smoking is perhaps the best example of how individual behavior can have a direct impact on health. Today, cigarette smoking is recognized as the single most important preventable cause of death in our society. It is responsible for more cancers and more cancer deaths than any other known agent; is a prime risk factor for heart and blood vessel disease, chronic bronchitis, and emphysema; and is a frequent cause of complications in pregnancies and of babies born prematurely, underweight, or with potentially fatal respiratory and cardiovascular problems.

Since the release of the Surgeon General's first report on smoking in 1964, the proportion of adult smokers has declined substantially, from 43% in 1965 to 30.5% in 1985. Since 1965, 37 million people have quit smoking. Although there is still much work to be done if we are to become a "smoke-free society," it is heartening to note that public health and public education efforts—such as warnings on cigarette packages and bans on broadcast advertising—have already had significant effects.

In 1835, Alexis de Tocqueville, a French visitor to America, wrote, "In America the passion for physical well-being is general." Today, as then, health and fitness are front-page items. But with the greater scientific and technological resources now available to us, we are in a far stronger position to make good health care available to everyone. And with the greater technological threats to us as we approach the 21st century, the need to do so is more urgent than ever before. Comprehensive information about basic biology, preventive medicine, medical and surgical treatments, and related ethical and public policy issues can help you arm yourself with the knowledge you need to be healthy throughout your life.

FOREWORD

Dale C. Garell, M.D.

A dvances in our understanding of health and disease during the 20th century have been truly remarkable. Indeed, it could be argued that modern health care is one of the greatest accomplishments in all of human history. In the early 20th century, improvements in sanitation, water treatment, and sewage disposal reduced death rates and increased longevity. Previously untreatable illnesses can now be managed with antibiotics, immunizations, and modern surgical techniques. Discoveries in the fields of immunology, genetic diagnosis, and organ transplantation are revolutionizing the prevention and treatment of disease. Modern medicine is even making inroads against cancer and heart disease, two of the leading causes of death in the United States.

Although there is much to be proud of, medicine continues to face enormous challenges. Science has vanquished diseases such as smallpox and polio, but new killers, most notably AIDS, confront us. Moreover, we now victimize ourselves with what some have called "diseases of choice," or those brought on by drug and alcohol abuse, bad eating habits, and mismanagement of the stresses and strains of contemporary life. The very technology that is doing so much to prolong life has brought with it previously unimaginable ethical dilemmas related to issues of death and dying. The rising cost of health care is a matter of central concern to us all. And violence in the form of automobile accidents, homicide, and suicide remains the major killer of young adults.

In the past, most people were content to leave health care and medical treatment in the hands of professionals. But since the 1960s, the consumer of medical care—that is, the patient—has assumed an increasingly central role in the management of his or her own health. There has also been a new emphasis placed on prevention: People are recognizing that their own actions can help prevent many of the conditions that have caused death and disease in the past. This accounts for the growing commitment to good nutrition and regular exercise, for the increasing number of people who are choosing not to smoke, and for a new moderation in people's drinking habits.

People want to know more about themselves and their own health. They are curious about their body: its anatomy, physiology, and biochemistry. They want to keep up with rapidly evolving medical technologies and procedures. They are willing to educate themselves about common disorders and diseases so that they can be full partners in their own health care.

THE ENCYCLOPEDIA OF HEALTH is designed to provide the basic knowledge that readers will need if they are to take significant responsibility for their own health. It is also meant to serve as a frame of reference for further study and exploration. The encyclopedia is divided into five subsections: The Healthy Body; The Life Cycle; Medical Disorders & Their Treatment; Psychological Disorders & Their Treatment; and Medical Issues. For each topic covered by the encyclopedia, we present the essential facts about the relevant biology; the symptoms, diagnosis, and treatment of common diseases and disorders; and ways in which you can prevent or reduce the severity of health problems when that is possible. The encyclopedia also projects what may lie ahead in the way of future treatment or prevention strategies.

The broad range of topics and issues covered in the encyclopedia reflects that human health encompasses physical, psychological, social, environmental, and spiritual well-being. Just as the mind and the body are inextricably linked, so, too, is the individual an integral part of the wider world that comprises his or her family, society, and environment. To discuss health in its broadest aspect it is necessary to explore the many ways in which it is connected to such fields as law, social science, public policy, economics, and even religion. And so, the encyclopedia is meant to be a bridge between science, medical technology, the world at large, and you. I hope that it will inspire you to pursue in greater depth particular areas of interest and that you will take advantage of the suggestions for further reading and the lists of resources and organizations that can provide additional information.

CHAPTER 1

THE TEETH

The Toothdrawer *by Gerard van Honthorst.*

From the onset of written history several thousand years ago, people have studied the teeth—their shape, their function, their loss—as well as their *restoration* after decay and other damage. Archaeologists have translated ancient Egyptian papyrus scrolls describing the treatment of teeth and other parts of the mouth. They have also read the works of the physician Celsus, who lived in ancient Rome from 23 B.C.

to A.D. 50 and wrote widely about various dental problems. In time, other doctors and scientists studied the teeth, and knowledge slowly developed about the structure and functions of these important body parts.

Early Dentistry

Until the start of modern dental practice in the 18th century, barber-surgeons handled most dental treatment. Called *dentatores* in 14th century France, where dentistry was the most advanced in the Western world, they pulled teeth, mostly to relieve pain, and performed many dental procedures known today.

The profession grew to include such procedures as scaling deposits from teeth and polishing them—a practice that had been followed by the early Greeks and Romans. Albucasis, an Arabian physician who lived from about 1050 to 1122, is now considered to have been the major dental surgeon of the Middle Ages. He designed a wide variety of scrapers for scaling teeth.

Pierre Fauchard is considered to be the founder of modern scientific dentistry. An 18th-century French practitioner, he wrote a monumental work entitled *The Surgeon Dentist: A Treatise on Teeth.* Fauchard and his colleagues worked in much the same way. They operated early drills by manually twisting the bur, or cutting bit, with one hand and operating the drill with the other.

By the mid-19th century, dentists, including those in the United States, had progressed in their profession. Some were primarily physicians who practiced dentistry as a sideline, whereas others were traveling, or itinerant, dental practitioners with very little professional training. They moved from town to town, extracting or filling teeth and constructing *dentures.* During those years, one could become a dentist by serving an apprenticeship of five years or so with an experienced practitioner.

At the start of the 1840s, though, experienced, qualified American dentists began teaching careers. One of them was Horace B. Hayden, a medical lecturer at the University of Baltimore College of Dental Surgery, which was the first dental college in the world. Modern

In this early European engraving, a blacksmith removes a woman's tooth. In medieval times, dentistry for the common people was left to blacksmiths and barbers.

dentistry has developed from these small beginnings. Today it takes a minimum of two to four years of college, followed by at least four years of study in one of the 55 dental schools in the United States to earn the generalist's, or dentist's, degree. Those who wish to specialize have to study another two to four years for the higher degree.

The first thing that aspiring young dental students learn when they enter dental school is the basic physical structure of the teeth. They study the two general kinds of teeth—the primary and the permanent. In addition, young dentists familiarize themselves with the various

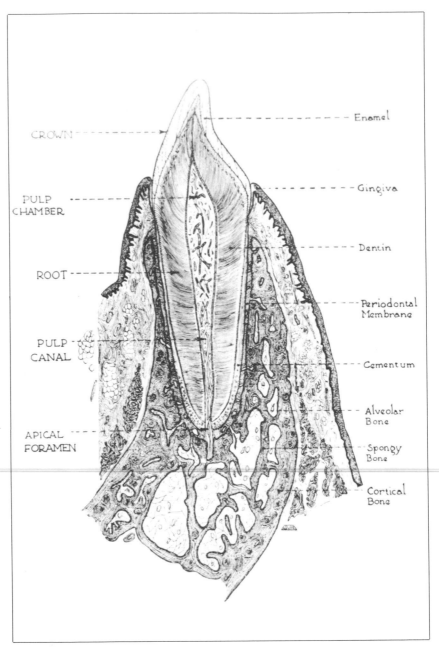

A medical illustrator's drawing of a tooth.

layers and parts of the teeth, ranging from the underlying support structure to the soft inner *pulp* and hard outer enamel. This basic knowledge is essential to a complete understanding of dental health.

The Primary Teeth

As soon as a sperm fertilizes an egg in a mother's body, it begins dividing into billions of cells that eventually form specific body parts. Some of these are teeth, which originate from the middle and outer layers of the embryo, or developing baby. In humans the teeth start forming about three weeks after conception. At about that time, a depression called the oral groove appears in the growing embryo and starts forming what will later be its mouth. Roughly three weeks later, when the embryo is less than half an inch long, certain cells of what has become the oral epithelium, or skin, gather into about 10 tiny, soft, irregular balls along the evolving jaw. This is the first appearance of the teeth, which, at this stage, are usually called tooth buds or germs. Newly formed blood vessels carry such minerals as calcium and phosphorus from foods the mother eats to help the buds develop.

Between the fourth and sixth months of pregnancy, the process of mineralization, or hardening, begins. Microscopic cells called ameloblasts start to grow out of the epithelium. They deposit a material that later calcifies into enamel, one of the body's hardest substances. The first teeth to appear are referred to variously as primary, baby, milk, or deciduous teeth.

At this stage of pregnancy, some of the primary teeth develop enamel *crown* tips, which are the first parts to form. They then erupt, or push through, the gums. Once the crown is completely grown and hard, the *root* starts to develop. When a tooth erupts, the crown is already complete, and the root is about two-thirds formed. Now the first permanent teeth also start to form.

A developing baby's first teeth erupt when it is six to eight months old. This is sometimes called eruption, or cutting teeth, but most often is referred to as teething. Female babies teethe a little earlier than male babies. But regardless of gender, the process continues for the follow-

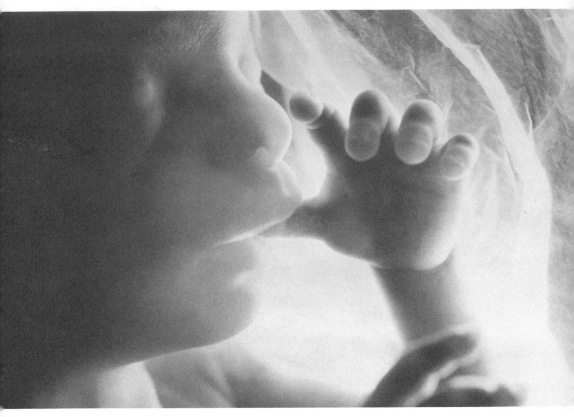

In humans teeth will start to form about three weeks after fertilization of the embryo.

ing two years. Generally, the two lower central teeth appear first, followed by the two upper central ones, with later lower teeth continuing to precede upper ones.

These first teeth are usually the central incisors. The next to appear are the lateral incisors, which come through just beside the central ones at nine months, and three to five months later the first molars erupt. At the age of 16 to 18 months, cuspids, also called canines or eye teeth, arrive to fill in the gap. Eventually, between the ages of 20 and 30 months, the child's final primary teeth, the second molars, erupt, marking the end of original teething. At the age of five or six years, the first permanent teeth, the six-year molars, arrive. Once all the primary teeth erupt they may appear to be strangely aligned, that is, to be turned or staggered in place. Before long, though, they will line up more or less neatly thanks to the molding pressure of baby's teeth and gums.

The Permanent Teeth

After early teething concludes, the child has a mouthful of 20 primary teeth. But he or she will eventually have 32 permanent teeth. These include three kinds of primary teeth—the incisors, the cuspids, and the molars—as well as a fourth type, the bicuspids, and four permanent third molars, or *wisdom teeth*. Before then, though, there will be gaps in the mouth as primary teeth fall out.

The permanent teeth lie just beneath the roots of the primary ones. As each permanent tooth grows, it presses on the roots of the primary one it will replace. The pressure causes the primary root to break down and start to resorb, or dissolve. Eventually, its roots disintegrate completely, and with nothing anchoring the first tooth in place, it falls out of the jaw. Often, children loosen a primary tooth by continually wiggling it with their tongue or fingers.

While the primary teeth do this disappearing act, the mouth prepares for the permanent teeth. Spaces begin to form between the front teeth, signalling that the jaws are growing to make room for the larger permanent teeth to come. During the period between the eruption of six-year molars and the replacement of the last primary tooth, the mouth is a mixture of both kinds of teeth. This is called the period of mixed dentition. Many dental professionals consider the six-year molars a child's most important teeth and, therefore, the cornerstones of the mouth.

Underlying Tooth Structure

Each tooth is composed of a crown, which projects above the gums, and a root, which is hidden by them. The tooth narrows at the neck, where the root and crown meet. The visible crown varies in shape, depending on the function of the tooth. Much of a tooth is formed by

The Toothpuller, *engraved by Andre Pauli after a painting by Theodor Rombouts.*

its root or roots. A canine tooth has a single root whereas a molar has two or three small ones fused together. Third molars may have as many as four or five roots.

A deep socket, the alveolus, anchors each tooth in place with the help of thin, strong connective fibers that form the *periodontal ligament.* These connective fibers fix teeth roots firmly to the jaw and attach the gums to the teeth. In addition, they are shock absorbers, protecting both jaws and teeth from damage that could be caused by the pressure of chewing. Generously supplied with myriad blood

vessels, nerves, and bone-building material, the periodontal ligament is an essential component in every tooth. As long as it remains healthy, it can continue nourishing the tooth and keep it alive.

The bony *alveolar process* is part of the jawbone that forms and supports each tooth socket. During replacement of primary teeth by permanent ones, the overlying root of each earlier tooth is absorbed as a fresh socket is produced for the permanent tooth that follows. The alveolar bone regularly undergoes pressure and tension with use. Consequently, it dissolves and reforms continuously. For instance,

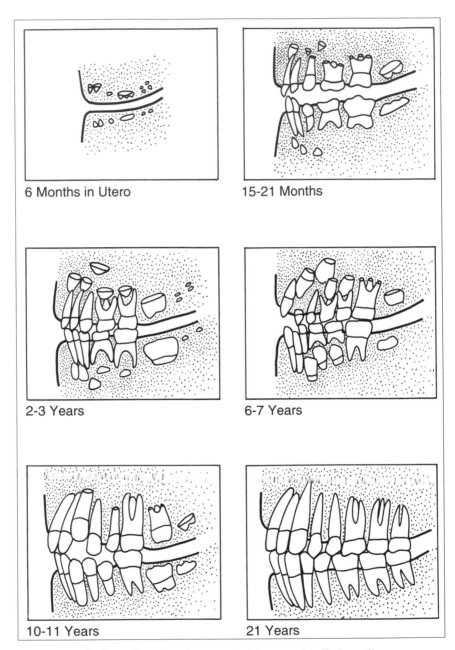

6 Months in Utero

15-21 Months

2-3 Years

6-7 Years

10-11 Years

21 Years

These panels show the development of human teeth from the prenatal period to adulthood.

when orthodontic work, or tooth realignment, moves a tooth into a new position, bone is absorbed at the socket's wall where pressure is applied.

Enamel

A shiny, tough, translucent substance called enamel covers all of the exposed teeth from the upper crown to the neck at the gum line. The hardest tissue produced by the body, enamel is composed of roughly 97% inorganic, or nonliving, material. So most of the tooth enamel is dead tissue. Consisting of calcium, phosphorus, and other minerals, enamel is sometimes referred to by dental professionals as "pearl" because it is not always white. In fact, tooth enamel varies in color, ranging from yellowish near the root to grayish white near the top of the crown. Much of its coloring depends upon its thickness and degree of calcification.

Being extremely hard, tooth enamel is meant to last, yet once formed, it cannot repair itself when damaged. When nails are chipped or bones broken, the body can help them to heal because they can still receive nourishment through the bloodstream. But once a fully developed tooth erupts, its enamel loses all contact with the blood supply and with any sources of nutrition that might help in the healing process. Isolated on the outside of a tooth, it has no repair cells. All that is left for the enamel to do is protect the layers lying underneath it from heat, cold, and the harmful sugars and acids found in every mouth.

Dentin, Pulp, and Cementum

Teeth are largely composed of *dentin,* the body's second hardest substance. It is yellowish in color and lies inside the crown and root. Although softer than enamel, dentin is similar to bone and is usually strong enough to support the hard outer enamel surface of the crown from within. Most important, dentin can repair itself. Composed of about 72% mineral salts, this layer is alive because the bloodstream nourishes the portion lying below the gum line, so it can mend itself when necessary. Millions of tiny tubes, sometimes called canals, carry important nourishment from the bloodstream to the inner dentin. The canals can also convey sensation, such as pain, from outside the tooth.

Dentin protects the innermost part of the tooth, called the pulp. As long as the pulp remains alive, dentin can reproduce itself. Especially important, dentin also provides the elasticity, or flexibility, needed for chewing. Without that, teeth would crack and break after taking several bites of a hard candy, bagel, or pretzel.

Dental pulp, often called the nerve, lies deep within each tooth in its special space—the *pulp chamber.* A jumble of soft grayish tissue holding tiny nerves and numerous small blood vessels, the pulp also contains branches of larger blood vessels and nerves. Extending through the opening at the end of every tooth, the pulp is connected to the main blood vessels and nerves within the jaw. At this point they join the blood and nerve system of the face and head. The pulp is one of the most vital elements of the entire body, because it gives life to each tooth.

The pulp's most important function is the production of new dentin inside the pulp chamber. Pulp responds to pressure from decay or from a deep *filling* by making new dentin, thus protecting itself from irritation. Pulp may be damaged by widespread decay, by a hard blow to the tooth, or by biting on extremely hard objects. Because pulp chambers in primary teeth are rather large in proportion to tooth size, they are more apt to be injured. However, pulp is quite tough and frequently repairs itself if the injury is not too severe.

Cementum, which meets the crown enamel at the neck of the tooth, is a covering that protects the root. Thin and bonelike, it differs from enamel in an important way: cementum is alive. Connected to the blood vessels in the jawbone, unlike enamel, it can repair itself after being damaged. Especially important, cementum directs nourishment to the rest of the tooth.

CHAPTER 2

HOW THE TEETH AND JAWS FUNCTION

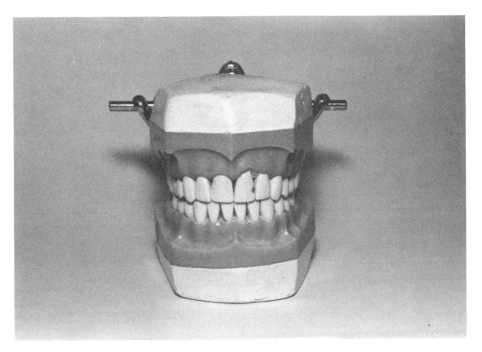

A model of human teeth.

The teeth function in three different ways. Most importantly, they prepare food for digestion by biting, cutting, chewing, and grinding it. They also play a major role in normal speech, which is why it is sometimes difficult to understand toothless adults when they speak. Finally, teeth influence facial appearance. If they protrude, are set too closely together, or are otherwise unsightly, they can damage self-esteem and be a social liability.

The Job of the Teeth

Dental experts consider the six-year molars the most important teeth in a child's mouth. The largest, strongest, and most useful of the rear teeth, they grind food into tiny bits to make them easier to swallow and digest. Indeed, children rely on them for chewing up to the time when many primary teeth fall out. Equally significant as cornerstones of the mouth and jaws, the six-year molars have the important job of guiding neighboring teeth into their proper places in front of and behind them. The second molars follow the six-year ones about six or seven years later.

Another kind of tooth, the incisors are named from the word *incise,* which means to cut. When the upper and lower incisors meet, they act like scissors, grasping and cutting off food particles. The word bicuspid describes a tooth that has two *cusps,* or pointed projections, that compose its chewing and biting surface. These teeth work with the cuspids in front of them to tear, shred, or partially crush the food the incisors have bitten off. Cuspids are so named because they have a single cusp, which is very long and sharp.

The third set of molars is called wisdom teeth. Four of them come in behind the second permanent molars. They usually appear between the ages of 16 and 21 and are labeled third molars because they are the third in the row of these teeth to grow. The term wisdom teeth seems related to the age at which they erupt—when people are expected to be wiser. Much less useful than the other molars, wisdom teeth are the smallest and weakest of the lot.

Because they are the last to arrive, wisdom teeth must fill in whatever space remains for them at the rear of the mouth. When this is especially limited, they may stay partially or completely embedded in the jawbone, in which case they are called *impacted teeth.* Although they might push in any direction, impacted teeth often grow forward and press against a neighboring molar. This can cause continuing pressure and pain. Severe pain may also occur when an impacted tooth decays below the gum's surface. Even without such discomfort, impacted wisdom teeth can cause other problems, such as crowding nearby teeth and forcing them out of line. Therefore, impacted third molars are often removed for the sake of dental health.

Chewing

"One of the most complicated and marvelous things the body does is chew," says A. Norman Cranin, former Director of Dental Services at the Brookdale Hospital Center in New York City. It is a process that involves *occlusion,* or biting, as the teeth in one jaw meet those in the

This photograph shows how a cast of teeth is made from a plaster mold of a real mouth.

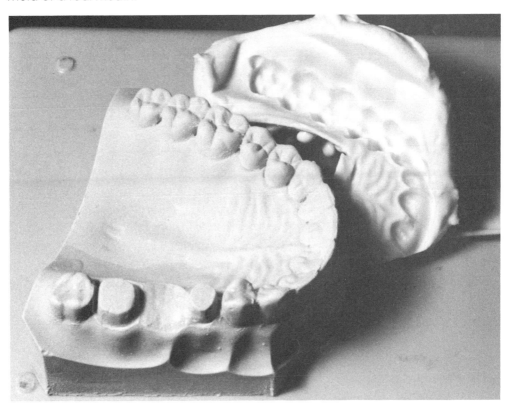

other. The United States Public Health Service has summed up the importance of "proper chewing" from early years: "A child needs sound baby teeth for proper chewing of the variety of foods which promote his growth. Correct chewing is the first step in good digestion without which the child's body cannot make full use of his food. This is vitally important because, in proportion to his weight, a child must eat three times the amount of food required by a grown person."

Clearly, a great deal depends upon proper chewing. Thoroughly chewed food is being prepared for digestion by the body through the specialized fluids it secretes, from gastric juices to saliva. Proper chewing also releases the substances—such as fats, protein, and starches—essential to good health, as well as such necessary nutrients as vitamins, minerals, hormones, and enzymes.

The chewing procedure does not necessarily come naturally. Young children do not master the art of chewing until they have all of their primary teeth. They have to make a major change, going from sucking to chewing, in the processing of food.

Sucking involves moving the tongue backward, whereas chewing requires a sideways movement. Also, the young child must learn to handle larger and harder pieces of food, judge how long to chew before swallowing, as well as how and when to close the lips. It is a more complex operation than one would imagine at first thought.

Chewing follows several steps. First, the eater takes a bite of food into his or her mouth. This triggers certain nerves into sending a variety of signals. For instance, the tongue, lips, and cheeks begin to steer food between the upper and lower teeth and, simultaneously, spurts of saliva moisten and partially digest it. This moistening is what makes food chewable. As the food is chewed, it breaks down into small pieces. Soon, it is ground and moistened enough to be taken over by the tongue, which sends it back against the hard palate. From there the food moves down the esophagus. Digestion has begun.

Speech

The teeth are just as important as aids to speech as they are in shaping the face and processing food through chewing. In order to speak

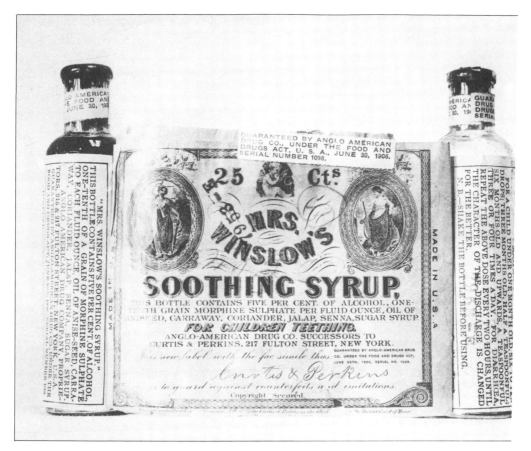

This label from a tooth pain remedy marketed in 1906 shows that morphine was used as an ingredient. The addictive nature of such substances was not clearly understood at the time.

properly people need correctly aligned teeth, which means that their teeth should be fairly straight, each tooth positioned in just the right way. Good speech begins with the eruption of the primary teeth. After the first molars appear, a child starts learning to imitate adult speech and usually by the age of two he or she has developed some vocabulary.

Teeth also help in the pronunciation of certain letters. For instance, the upper front teeth are essential in pronouncing *F* and *V.* When the lower lips press against the edges of the upper incisors, they form those sounds. On the other hand, as the tongue curves toward the edges of

the upper front teeth, it makes the sounds of the letters *C, S, X,* and *Z.*
To pronounce the combination of *th,* as in *thank* or *think,* the tip of the
tongue is lifted to the edge of the upper teeth.

It should be obvious by now how difficult clear speech would be if
the teeth were missing. Rapid recital of "Peter Piper picked a peck of
pickled peppers" would be impossible without the incisors. And severe
malocclusion—the condition in which the teeth do not fit together
correctly when the jaws are closed—also affects speech. Further, the
positioning of teeth usually influences the way people feel about
themselves. When someone has difficulty speaking, due in part to tooth
misalignment, loss of self-confidence often follows, along with related

*This plaster cast reveals an overbite, a common malocclusion where
the patient's teeth do not properly fit together, and the grinding of
food is less efficient.*

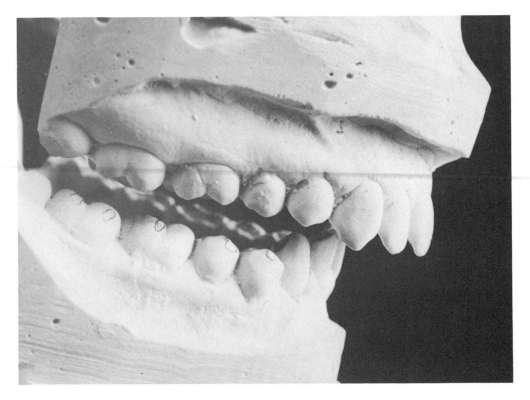

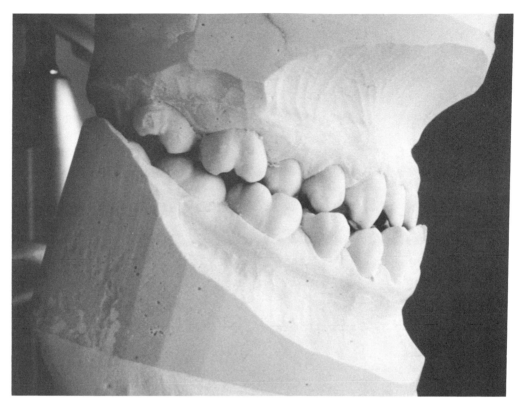

Another malocclusion revealing an underbite.

personal problems. Poorly positioned, aligned, or spaced teeth can make a person's speech sound strange, causing such problems as a nasal tone or whistling sounds.

The Jaws

When considering oral and dental health, people tend to consider the teeth alone. Although vital to nutrition, speech, and appearance, they are only one of the structures in the mouth. In fact, the teeth would be useless without the other structures on which they depend.

As the mouth's supportive structure, the jawbone is the anchor of all teeth and thus the very foundation of oral health. Human jawbones have evolved over thousands of years, starting as gill arches in the mouths of primitive fish. Now, human jawbones support the *dental arch*—the complete set of teeth in the mouth. The jaw has a two-part structure: the *maxilla,* or upper jaw, and the *mandible,* or lower jaw.

Everyone's head is divided into two parts—the skull and the face. The upper jawbone is fixed to both face and skull and cannot move. The lower jaw is the only movable bone in the head. Suspended from the skull by the temporomandibular joint on each side and in front of the ear, it is controlled by very large, strong muscles. The two masseter muscles, set in the angle of the lower jaw, raise and lower it during chewing. Another series of muscles, called muscles of mastication, also help make the jaw move. They fan out in various directions, attaching to specific places along the surrounding skull structures as well as the inner regions of the neck and throat. The muscles of mastication move only by contracting, or shortening, in response to signals from the nervous system. The muscles are balanced in opposing pairs, so when one pair gets a signal to open or shorten, its opposites receive a signal to let go in order to stretch.

Teeth should lie closely together in both the maxillary and mandibular arches. To function properly, they must occlude. In other words, when the jaws are closed, the upper and lower teeth should mesh together approximately evenly. The place where this occurs is called the line of occlusion, or bite. A complementary structure is the dental ridge, a bony, tissue-covered support for teeth in the lower or upper arch. When teeth are lost, it becomes the support for dentures. Other wise, facial appearance could be drastically affected.

Permanent teeth are meant to last a lifetime. In a sense, as the child's face grows and expands, it makes up for the temporary loss of teeth. Lacking this kind of cushion, the adult face is more vulnerable. When a permanent tooth is lost, it is gone forever and nothing grows in to take its place. The older the adult, the more serious this can be because tooth or teeth loss can significantly change the way a person's face looks. Incisors and canines in particular directly support the shape of the lips, corners of the mouth, and front parts of the cheeks. The older the adult, the more sunken the face can become after tooth loss.

A teenage girl wearing braces on her teeth to correct a malocclusion.

The Gums

Every tooth is surrounded by firm, padded, light pink or coral-colored tissue. This is the gum, also called *gingiva,* which has the job, along with the roots of the teeth, of holding the teeth in place. Covering the jaws inside the mouth, gums surround each tooth base and fill in the spaces between the teeth. Until late adolescence, a protective membrane normally attaches gums to the teeth. That membrane disappears from the older mouth, and, therefore, adults often have empty spaces just under the gums where bits of food may easily become trapped. Gingiva tissue is very tough and strong because the gums undergo stresses and strains caused by chewing. When healthy, the gums cannot be damaged so easily.

CHAPTER 3

DENTAL PROBLEMS

A photograph of a dentist's office in 1908, showing one early method of coping with dental pain.

Some of the most common dental problems are related to tooth decay. Dental *caries*, or *cavities*, can form in teeth, causing tooth deterioration and often considerable pain. Various injuries to the jaw are also common problems dealt with by dentists. Treating decay or jaw injury promptly is essential to good dental health.

Cavities

A dental cavity is simply a hole in a tooth or tooth surface. It is caused by decay, which can travel down into the tooth, to the dentin and, in a worst case scenario, into the pulp.

In the 1950's, researchers at the National Institute of Dental Research, or NIDR, a division of the National Institutes of Health, demonstrated that tooth decay is caused by dental *plaque,* a sticky, bacteria-laden film that builds up around the teeth and gums. Plaque also accumulates in the pits and grooves of the back molars. Although it may adhere to other teeth, these are the teeth it affects most often, mainly because it is often hard to reach them with a toothbrush.

The primary bacteria in dental plaque are *Streptococcus mutans.* In a process called demineralization, these bacteria convert refined sugar and starch in the foods we eat into lactic and other organic acids, which, in turn, dissolve the calcium salts that make up most of the tooth enamel. All of this can start within half an hour of the time the foods enter the mouth, even when teeth are otherwise healthy.

The first electric drill.

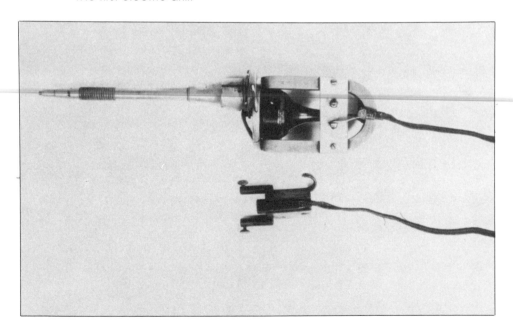

The sticky nature of plaque enables bacteria and their acids to stay on the tooth surfaces instead of being washed away by saliva. The longer plaque remains undisturbed, the greater its ability to produce harmful acids. Moreover, when plaque is not removed daily with thorough brushing, it accumulates and hardens into a gritty substance called calculus, or tartar, which can only be removed in a dental office.

Because of the way they grow, six-year molars often develop cavities once they erupt. When a tooth starts growing, it forms into several points. At first they are separate and distinct. But as the tooth hardens, the points unite at the base to make a complete tooth crown. Quite often all parts of a tooth do not join perfectly. Even when the tooth is fully developed, tiny cracks and holes may remain. Food catches in those gaps where toothbrushes cannot reach them and decay soon starts. In fact, about 90% of all new permanent molars have these imperfections. Because six-year molars are probably the most frequently lost permanent teeth, it is essential that a dentist check them as soon as they appear. Only a professional can detect tiny cracks and holes. He or she can fill them and prepare them for a lifetime of health.

Toothache

The Roman physician Celsus called toothache "among the worst of tortures." No one who has ever suffered this kind of oral pain would disagree. Celsus only suspected the causes of toothache, whereas modern dentists know that such pain is often related to cavities. But not always. For instance, toothache can originate with food trapped between the teeth. This then irritates the gums, which send forth messages of pain. It is what the experts term "low grade" discomfort. Indeed, in such cases it is the gingiva and supporting tissue rather than the tooth that is affected. The solution is quite simple: vigorous brushing and rinsing of the mouth, followed by careful flossing to remove trapped food.

But there is another type of toothache that is not as easily cured, one that involves continuous pain. Dental practitioners can often predict its course. The worst case scenario mentioned earlier, in which decay reaches down through dental layers to the pulp, will often cause almost unbearable, throbbing pain. This is because pulpal nerves respond quite strongly to pain stimuli. A really deep cavity or a tooth fracture can cause an *abscess,* or pulp infection, to form, with excruciatingly painful symptoms. Pain, accompanied by swelling, nearly always indicates pulp infection.

A tooth fracture could be a hairline crack. A tooth that seems healthy occasionally develops such a break, which causes severe pain. Yet the problem is hard to diagnose even after X rays are taken, because such

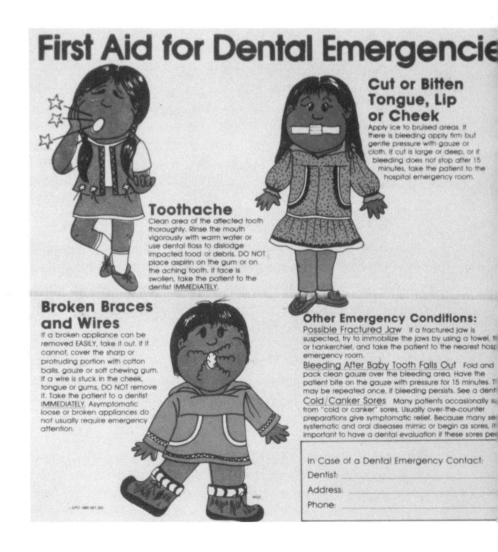

First Aid for Dental Emergencie

Cut or Bitten Tongue, Lip or Cheek

Apply ice to bruised areas. If there is bleeding apply firm but gentle pressure with gauze or cloth. If cut is large or deep, or if bleeding does not stop after 15 minutes, take the patient to the hospital emergency room.

Toothache

Clean area of the affected tooth thoroughly. Rinse the mouth vigorously with warm water or use dental floss to dislodge impacted food or debris. DO NOT place aspirin on the gum or on the aching tooth. If face is swollen, take the patient to the dentist IMMEDIATELY.

Broken Braces and Wires

If a broken appliance can be removed EASILY, take it out. If it cannot, cover the sharp or protruding portion with cotton balls, gauze or soft chewing gum. If a wire is stuck in the cheek, tongue or gums, DO NOT remove it. Take the patient to a dentist IMMEDIATELY. Asymptomatic loose or broken appliances do not usually require emergency attention.

Other Emergency Conditions:

Possible Fractured Jaw If a fractured jaw is suspected, try to immobilize the jaws by using a towel, ti or hankerchief, and take the patient to the nearest hosp emergency room.

Bleeding After Baby Tooth Falls Out Fold and pack clean gauze over the bleeding area. Have the patient bite on the gauze with pressure for 15 minutes. T may be repeated once. If bleeding persists. See a dent

Cold/Canker Sores Many patients occasionally su from "cold or canker" sores. Usually over-the-counter preparations give symptomatic relief. Because many se systematic and oral diseases mimic or begin as sores, it important to have a dental evaluation if these sores per

In Case of a Dental Emergency Contact:

Dentist: _____

Address: _____

Phone: _____

cracks simply may not show up on them. However, if a dentist suspects fracture-related infection he or she might prescribe treatment with an antibiotic such as penicillin, which is usually effective. Should this treatment fail, different, more complex, therapy will be attempted, for a dentist's prime goals are relief for the patient and saving the tooth.

As indicated earlier, third molars, or wisdom teeth, can be troublesome in terms of forcing neighboring teeth out of line. But they can also pose a different threat: infection due to the impaction. One of the

This chart teaches youngsters how to cope with simple dental emergencies.

most common types of infection is percoronitis, or infection around a tooth crown. When a flap of gum tissue lies around the slowly erupting tooth, food and bacteria can be trapped between the top of the crown and the tissue. The result is pain, accompanied by bone infection. Impacted third molars can cause other problems, among them *resorption,* or the dissolving of the root of an adjoining tooth under gradual pressure. Even when third molars erupt unhindered, a patient's problems are not necessarily over. Because these teeth are set so far back in the jaw, even the most diligent tooth brushing may not reach them. Understandably, many dental practitioners feel that for the reasons just cited, it is often wise to extract wisdom teeth at the first sign of trouble.

Trauma

Another cause of dental pain is trauma, or injury, stemming from damage to the face, teeth, and jawbone. The NIDR reports that automobile accidents remain the most common cause of skull and facial trauma. Other causes are fire, falls, bicycle accidents, and sports injuries. Among the latter, football, soccer, boxing, hockey, and barefisted fights commonly lead to traumatic injury. In such cases, teeth may be broken or knocked out. When a tooth is knocked out during a sports event, it should be swiftly replaced in its socket and held in place with the tongue or clean fingers. Then the patient should be rushed to a dentist's office. The first half hour is critical. If much more than 30 minutes elapses, the root is apt to be absorbed, or eaten away, by the body.

More serious injuries require the services of an oral surgeon. If a driver's face hits the steering wheel in an accident, there may be a combination of crushed flesh, loosened or lost teeth, and a broken or fractured jaw. In other words, the kind of facial deformation a surgeon usually treats in the hospital. In cases such as these, the first step is to assess the damage. For example, in the case of a fractured jawbone the doctor makes a diagnosis by visual examination and X ray. If bones are broken but still in alignment, it is a simple fracture and treatment is also simple. Lower teeth are merely wired to the upper ones to immoblize the jaw, a technique dating from ancient times. Healing takes about six weeks, during which the patient "eats" a liquid diet high in protein and carbohydrates fortified with vitamins. After the wires are removed the patient can chew normally.

On the other hand, a more severe accident could cause serious disfigurement. In a compound fracture, at the very least a part of the bone sticks through the skin of the face or membranes of the mouth. There can also be tiny bone fragments in the mouth, which are discarded before treatment begins. Stereoscopic X rays are taken, adding

These devices were used to extract teeth around 1850.

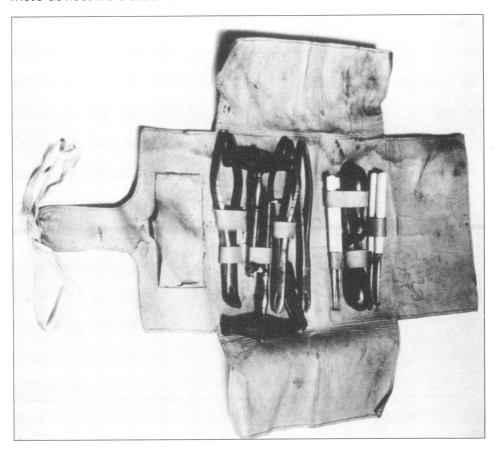

a third dimension so that the specialist can "see" the full damage. In such cases the bones are often manually repositioned, under anesthesia, in a process called reducing the fracture. Sometimes rubber bands or other elastic, or flexible, traction help accomplish this. Once the parts are aligned, the jaws are wired together as with simple fractures. In both fracture cases, the wires act much the way a plaster cast does when immobilizing broken limbs.

Other Therapies for Jaw Damage

In classical Greece, Hippocrates (*circa* 460–377 B.C.), often called the father of medicine, described a similar way of treating jaw fractures: tying together rigid teeth lying next to the break with linen cords. Later, Romans used gold wire for this purpose. Today, oral surgeons use more sophisticated therapies. Wearing the two hats of dentist and surgeon, they know just how teeth should relate to each other when they repair fractures.

Oral surgeons treat more than just the teeth, however. For example, they help patients who may have oral cancer by performing biopsies, studies that can identify malignant, or cancerous tissue. If the tests are positive, the oral surgeon carries out treatment, which could mean removal of a jaw part or the roof of the mouth. This is a serious procedure and can be frightening to the patient, but it is often the only way to save a patient's life.

Later, the surgeon can assist in facial reconstruction. Dr. Howard Siegeler, an oral surgeon who practices in Fair Lawn, New Jersey, has rebuilt missing jawbones using bone grafts as well as synthetic, or artificial, materials. "First of all," he says, "the bone graft itself is usually done by autogenous bone [that is] from the same patient." It could come from the ribs or pieces of the hipbone. Often, the procedure is carried out in conjunction with a general or orthopedic surgeon. The latter specializes in treating diseases of the bones and joints. "It all depends on the extent of the surgery," Dr. Siegeler adds. The possibilities range from "massive cancer surgery . . . removal of the jaws . . . to what they call a commando procedure, which is the removal of the mandible [lower jaw] and neck dissections for cancers in that area."

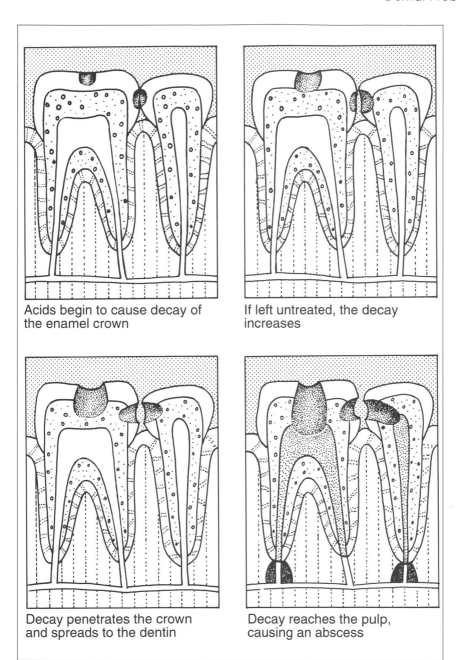

Acids begin to cause decay of the enamel crown

If left untreated, the decay increases

Decay penetrates the crown and spreads to the dentin

Decay reaches the pulp, causing an abscess

These drawings show the progress of tooth decay from the beginning of a cavity to the development of an abscess.

In autogenous graft operations, says Siegeler, bone parts "are often shaped right on the site by an orthopedic surgeon or some kind of head and neck surgeon who does the reconstruction." If a patient cannot supply bone parts, there are other options. For example, bone banks in California keep small sections of freeze-dried human and bovine, or cattle, bone as possible transplant material. These are specially treated to remove anything that might cause rejection by the body or introduce disease. Then they can be used to build up small defects, Dr. Siegeler explains, "such as tooth sockets in periodontal disease." Thus, specialists have real bone to pack into spaces left after surgical removal of jaw parts. These form "a beginning area." Then, if any living bone-producing cells remain, they can interact with the new matter which will eventually become bony.

Further, according to Dr. Siegeler, there are "outside products which are not bone . . . and not human in nature." One of these, hydroxyapatite, is an enzyme in pellet form. Developed by oral surgeons, it is a substance chemically similar to bone and, therefore, especially useful in graft procedures. After being resorbed by the body, it stimulates bone growth on its own. "There are also non-resorbable [things] that are used simply to build up shape," he continues. "For instance, if a patient had a mandible without teeth, and this mandible was atrophic [wasting away], or was very small . . . and he couldn't wear dentures because there was no [ridge] to build on, there are ways to build up that ridge . . . using these non-resorbable pellets. They are literally injected under the gum. That way the gum can be shaped and "really give shape to the ridge itself." When a denture is built on top of this new ridge, there is a dramatic change in the patient's appearance.

CHAPTER 4

BASIC DENTAL THERAPY

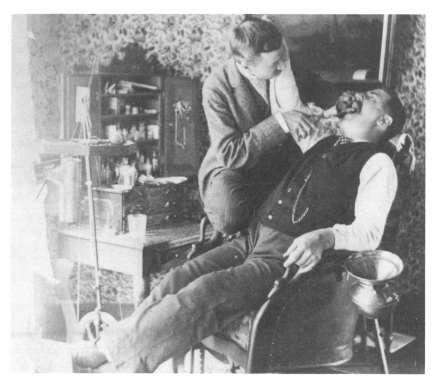

A turn of the century stereopticon slide shows a dentist trying to remove a particularly stubborn tooth. For a field of medicine associated with so much pain, dentistry has been the butt of much humor.

In ancient Rome, doctors, much like today's dentists, drilled into teeth, filled cavities, and made necessary *extractions*. They also used gold crowns to restore teeth and replaced missing ones largely for appearance. These were practical men, and when confronted with oral problems they tried to cure them. But their scientific understanding was primitive. For instance, they believed a tooth worm caused dental caries.

They had no idea that plaque causes decay, which, if not halted, travels swiftly through a tooth until the pulp is threatened. The only thing that can stop such decay, modern dentists know, is a filling.

Fillings

X rays reveal a cavity's location in a tooth so that a dentist can treat or fill it. The first step is choosing a filling material. For a simple cavity that is not very large, especially when the filling will show when the patient smiles, most dentists choose porcelain, a mixture of tooth-colored substances also called composite filling materials.

But when the filling will not show, dentists often use a substance known as amalgam. A mix of about 70% silver and 30% tin, copper, zinc, and mercury, amalgam is also called a silver filling. In 1895, after years of experimentation, Dr. C. V. Black of Chicago introduced the amalgam mixture, which has hardly changed since. Before then, dental practitioners had filled teeth with such varied materials as gold foil, which did not last very long, and cobwebs. According to the American Dental Association, or ADA, 75% of all single-tooth restorations today are amalgams.

Having chosen the filling material, the dentist prepares the tooth. Undoubtedly, the cavity still contains decayed food and germs. These must be removed, and the hole thoroughly cleaned to prevent additional decay. Then the opening has to be shaped so that the filling will remain in place after insertion. Different drills clean out the cavity. A low-speed one is best for children because greater speed cuts too fast for small teeth. The high-speed water-cooled drill usually prepares adult teeth for fillings. A drill uses any of an assortment of small cutters called burs. Made of carbine steel or bonded diamond particles on a steel shank, they clean out cavities and polish finished fillings.

If there is any possibility of pain during this procedure, the dentist uses an anesthetic beforehand. Dental anesthetics of one kind or another have been around for a long time. In ancient Rome, doctors used such natural drugs as opium poppy and mandrake, a member of the nightshade family, to alleviate pain. Each acted as a narcotic. Later, a 14th-century surgeon, Guy de Chauliac, described how colleagues soaked a sponge in the juices of mandrake root then left it to dry in the sun. Before an operation, the sponge would be dipped in warm water, then held under a patient's nose until he or she fell asleep. This worked so well, de Chauliac wrote, that the surgeon could awaken his patient only by holding another sponge, this time soaked in vinegar, under his or her nose.

Modern dental anesthesia did not appear until the middle of the 19th century. Dr. Horace Wells of Hartford, Connecticut, introduced ether into his dental practice in 1864. Two years earlier, Dr. Thomas W. Evans of Philadelphia began promoting nitrous oxide as a dental anesthetic. He lectured about his discovery in England throughout the 1860s, and nitrous oxide is still widely used in that country.

Though they have come a long way in 400 years, dental instruments can still be frightening to patients.

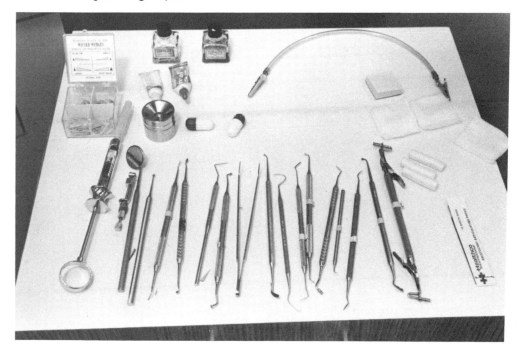

*An autoclave,
used to sterilize
dental instruments.*

Today, in the United States, many dentists use injected liquid anesthetics. First, a kind of salve is rubbed onto the gum to deaden sensation. Shortly afterward a needle shoots painkiller into the gum—usually Xylocaine, which has largely replaced the once widely used Novocain. Most often, the patient feels only a light prick.

Once the anesthetic takes effect and work on the cavity can begin, the dentist uses several other tools. A *saliva ejector* rests in the patient's mouth, keeping it dry as the drill works. It sucks up saliva, together

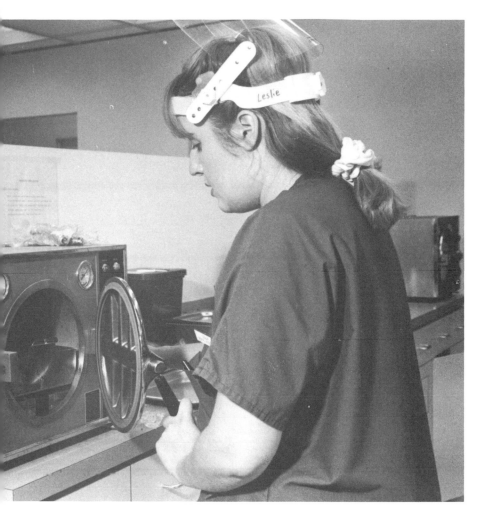

with streams of water from the high-speed drill. Water cools the tooth as the bur whirls against cavity walls. Without it, heat created by the bur could injure a tooth's nerve.

When wholly free of decay, the cavity can be filled. The amalgam is mixed, then inserted into the prepared hole. For a few minutes afterward, the patient sits quietly, mouth open, so the filling can dry. After it has begun to harden, the dentist trims the filling to fit the form of adjoining teeth. The entire restoration process is then complete.

Crowns, Caps, and Jackets

Some restorations replace seriously damaged teeth. These could be chipped, badly broken, or cracked. Whatever their state, many dentists say, where there is life, there is hope. Here, "life" means a remaining live root and a strong possibility of saving the tooth, thus restoring its natural appearance and function. This can be achieved with an artificial crown, also called a cap or a jacket. Fitted over the damaged tooth, a crown can look as natural, feel as comfortable, and work as well as a normal, healthy one.

There are several types of crowns, made of various materials and used on different teeth. Natural-looking porcelain jacket crowns go over the front teeth. Worn by many models, film stars, and other people in the public eye, the best crowns usually look like real teeth. Because of its great strength, the all-cast-gold crown is probably the most lasting. However, due to its color, it cannot be used for visible front teeth. The post-and-core crown is used after a nerve has been removed during *root canal therapy.* In such cases a tooth could eventually become brittle, so the post is used to provide more support and strength in the devitalized, or nerveless, tooth.

For restoration, the tooth being saved must be reduced in size. This is achieved through cutting away decay or other damage. In the process, even bits of sound tooth might be trimmed off. Dentists call this procedure tooth reduction or preparation. It reduces the chewing, or occlusal, surface to allow for the thickness of material used in the crown.

Once preparation is completed, the dentist uses an impression tray chosen from an assortment of shapes and sizes for either the upper or lower jaw. A puttylike material is placed in the tray, and the patient bites where directed, leaving an impression of the tooth being restored, as well as of the teeth in front of and behind it. When the material hardens to a rubbery consistency, it is removed from the mouth. The practitioner or dental assistant then takes a similar impression of the opposing tooth and its neighbors. A bite impression is also made by having the patient bite into a warmed piece of wax, thus showing how opposing teeth relate to each other. The dentist sends these materials to a dental laboratory, together with a notation of the color of the tooth being restored. Both dentist and lab technician have standard shade guides of normal tooth colors. If, for instance, the dentist wants a fairly white crown, an A-1 porcelain is ordered.

Crowns are usually made in variations of a single technique. In the case of the porcelain cap, for instance, a technician in the lab makes dies, or molds, from each impression with a special kind of material, usually a carbon-free phosphate. He or she puts a little metal thimble onto the model, where it acts as an undercasting. As one technician, Don Gregor of Borden Dental Laboratories of Hawthorne, New Jersey, explains, technicians use the model "as a reference to what [the patient] had." Then they duplicate the original, or natural, crown. With one die they make the crown base in whatever alloy the dentist specifies, often a silver-palladium or a nonprecious alloy, such as nickel-chromium or gold, on the thimble.

Next, the technician makes certain tests before going on to construct a crown. He or she mounts models of the tooth being restored and its opposite on a special mechanical device called an articulator, which mimics the jaw's biting movements. When the models occlude properly, the technician will start building the crown. After combining powdered porcelain with distilled water, he or she applies the mixture to the mold with a small spatula or artists' brushes. Starting with a cone shape, the technician builds it into something that roughly resembles a tooth but about 10% larger. This allows for shrinkage during the final baking, or firing, in a vacuum chamber within a small oven, where the temperature is set for about 1800° Fahrenheit. Porcelain and metal fuse during the baking. After the "tooth" cools off, the technician uses a special diamond high-speed hand piece to finish the shaping process, ending with a glaze coating and a final firing at 900° Fahrenheit. Gregor estimates that the entire process takes 12 to 14 steps.

Prosthodontics

A crown is a type of prosthetic device. Prosthetics is the branch of surgery dealing with the replacement of a body part with an artificial substitute. Dentists who specialize in prosthetic devices are known as prosthodontists. The modern use of prosthetics follows a long tradition. Archaeologists have excavated remarkable dental appliances made by ancient Egyptians and Phoenicians. They have also dug up dental bridges very much like modern ones made by the Etruscans, a people who lived in Italy in early Roman times. Especially important, Etruscan skeletal jaw specimens have been found with those bridges still in place.

Many years afterward, the practice of tooth replacement came to the English colonies in North America. Indeed, many prominent colo-

Dental X rays, seen here against a light table, reveal cavities and previous fillings and make the modern dentist's work easier and safer.

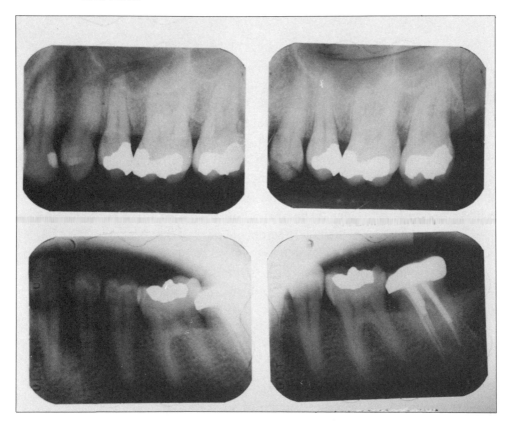

nial dentists treated George Washington. For most of his adult life, Washington suffered from serious toothaches and gradually lost most of his teeth. By 1790, at his first inauguration, only one tooth remained, a lower left bicuspid. As Washington lost his teeth, artificial replacements were made for him from a wide variety of materials. In fact, Dr. John Greenwood of New York City fashioned four sets of dentures for the first U.S. president out of such varied materials as gold, elephant ivory, and human teeth. The popular story that Washington's artificial teeth were made of wood has never been proven.

Today, besides crowns, other dental prosthetic devices include bridges that replace one or more teeth, as well as fixed or removable devices, popularly known as dentures. Bridges are a series of crowns and *pontics,* or tooth replacements, soldered together into a single unit. They are often called partials because they replace only part of a dental arch. Dentures usually replace most or all of the dental arch.

Immediate dentures may be best over the long term. They are put in place right after complete tooth extraction, but only after the dental ridge has healed. They are constructed before extractions are carried out in much the same way as crowns are made. In other words, impressions are taken of the existing teeth and ridges, wax replicas are made of those structures, jaw relationships are measured, and so on. The patient tries on the wax model, or models, to check looks and fit, after which it is sent to the lab for final construction of the denture.

The Final Restoration: Root Canal Therapy

Yet another kind of restoration can return badly damaged teeth to life. This is root canal therapy.

A root canal is the narrow, hollow chamber in a tooth's root. Sometimes trouble occurs in the root canal. For instance, bacteria from a deep cavity can infect the root, or a sudden blow to the jaw might damage the nerves and blood vessels. Also, severe decay or gum disease might affect the pulp.

Bacteria that cause infection can spread throughout the entire pulp, eventually reaching the jawbone. One symptom of diseased pulp is

A modern high-speed dentist's drill.

pain. As another symptom, the tooth can become extremely sensitive to hot or cold foods and drinks. Even without discomfort, the pulp may deteriorate gradually. Then the problem only appears during an X-ray examination, which is an important reason for regular dental check-ups.

Assuming that X rays reveal this trouble, the practitioner will treat the pulp before prescribing drastic measures, such as extraction, or removal. In fact, root canal therapy can save the tooth and restore it to health. It is relatively simple and takes at least two steps: swiftly removing the damaged pulp and then sterilizing and filling the canal. First, of course, the dentist determines whether the nerve has been destroyed. If it is still vital, or alive, a local anesthetic will help prevent possible discomfort. Treatment may require several visits to the dentist before he or she is satisfied that the canal has been cleared of infection. A temporary filling protects it from germs between visits. Then the canal and pulp chamber are filled, often with a rubberlike substance called gutta-percha.

Dental professionals estimate that root canal therapy succeeds in 90% to 95% of cases. But when a tooth cannot be restored, it may have to be removed.

Extraction

Teeth are pulled for various reasons. If, for example, root canal therapy fails, the dentist has no other recourse, and extraction becomes the last resort. Or a tooth may be too diseased to be saved, raising the possibility of infection spreading to other teeth or through the entire body. Other reasons for extraction include cases where a tooth rests precariously in diseased gum tissue or when it has received such a serious blow that an abscess forms. And when impacted wisdom teeth become particularly troublesome, they, too, are extracted for the reasons cited earlier.

Albucasis, an Arabian dental surgeon of the Middle Ages, wrote that extraction can be relatively simple and painless. He was right. Quite often it requires only two types of instruments, although each can vary in size and shape. The first is a forceps, which resembles a pair of pliers. Indeed, a forceps operates like pliers, grasping and holding a tooth along its root, just below the crown. Firmly in this grip, the tooth is rocked and rotated until it is loosened enough to come out along the path of least resistance. The second tool, an elevator, is used less often, largely to help pull seriously decayed teeth, broken parts of teeth, or impacted teeth.

After the extraction is completed, a hole remains where the tooth grew, and there may be bleeding from the wound. Until a replacement fills that gap, the patient can do several things to ease any discomfort and hasten the healing process. Normally, the body starts this by forming a blood clot to close the socket that once held the tooth. The

A technician checks the fit of a bridge, a set of three replacement teeth, on a cast taken from a patient's mouth.

clot also seals the socket to keep out germs, saliva, and food particles. Clots are major factors in capping off bleeding, and clot formation should not take more than a few minutes. To prevent complications, doctors usually advise patients to avoid strenuous activity, as well as hot liquids, for at least five or six hours, so that the clot will form and harden. If swelling occurs, an ice bag placed on the face where the operation was performed usually helps.

Implants, Transplants, and Replants

Restoration with crowns and the like can succeed only when there is some life left in a tooth. If not, the only answer may be a complete replacement of the original tooth with an implant, replant, or transplant. According to clinical studies from the NIDR, implants should function successfully without attachment to natural teeth, for they are really permanently attached false teeth that usually operate like natural ones.

Dr. Robert A. Jaffin, a periodontist with Affiliated Periodontists of North Jersey, in Hackensack, New Jersey, and a visiting professor at Temple University, Philadelphia, performs implant therapy. In fact, he and his partner, Dr. Charles Berman, have done 2,000 implants over an eight-year period. "Basically," he explains, "today the most predictable implants are little cylinders . . . or screw-shaped cylinders." Made of commercially-pure titanium covered with hydroxyapatite—the same material used to rebuild jaws—they were developed by a Swedish orthopedist named Branemark, "whose implants still seem to be state of the art," Dr. Jaffin says. Implants are made in much the same way as artificial crowns. The dentist takes a mouth impression and sends it to the lab where a false tooth is made on the titanium screw. Later, the dentist cements it to a metal post in the gum tissue.

In use since 1965, implants have had an impressive success rate. Dr. Jaffin finds that after the first year of insertion a "steady state" is usually reached. Indeed, he says, the loss of implants during the first year "is very low." He and Dr. Berman report a loss rate of only 4% in their patients.

The procedures require a sterile oral environment, in other words, a mouth cleaned of *periodontal* disease or other problems. The implant has to be set in "very gently," Dr. Jaffin says, "because if you [injure] the bone, you're killing bone cells, and the implant won't work." Given those conditions, Dr. Jaffin concludes, "implants work predictably," replacing anything from a single tooth up to an entire dental arch.

The price of this procedure depends on the number of teeth involved. It takes just about as much time to implant one tooth as it does three or four, and, therefore, should cost about the same for both operations. For example, a single implant can cost about $2,000. But a dental arch replacement would be $1,500 per implant. Dr. Jaffin explains: "For the lower jaw you only need five implants to do the entire line of jaw . . . figure on ten or twelve teeth for the implants in the lower [arch]." But bone in the upper jaw is a little softer, so more implants generally are needed there. "You have to think of an implant as a footing, or an area of support," he adds. "You only need a certain amount of these footings to build a bridge."

Replantation and implantation of teeth are somewhat similar procedures, carried out for related reasons. For instance, a tooth may have been knocked out accidentally or removed intentionally for surgery on its *apex*. In either case it can be replaced in its socket as described earlier. Should the procedure follow an accident, though, success is most likely when the tooth has been out of the mouth no longer than half an hour. If the dentist feels that it can be saved, he or she will reinsert the tooth using splints to hold it in position until it has a chance to reattach itself. This is a fairly simple, often painless operation that works most effectively on children's teeth. The replanted tooth becomes firmly attached within a short time and then functions normally.

In general, the results of implants and replants are much the same. However, for various reasons, such as infection and dissolving away of parts of the jawbone, failures may occur. Transplantation is the obvious next step. Here, a natural tooth replaces a lost one. This can be done with either a tooth from the same patient, called an autogenic transplant, or with another person's tooth, known as an allogenic transplant. The success rate depends on possible infection during and

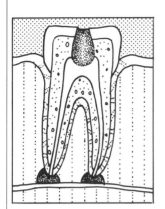

Decay has caused an abscess in the tooth

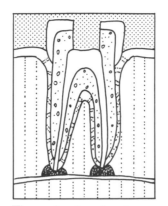

The pulp chamber is exposed by making an opening in the crown

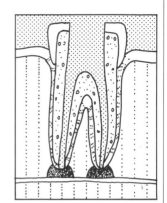

The pulp and the nerve are removed and the root canals are cleaned and enlarged

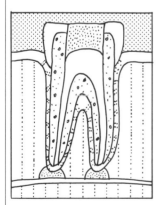

The dentist fills the root canals

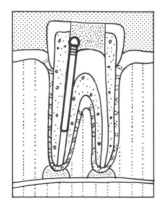

A metal post is often inserted in the root canal for structural support

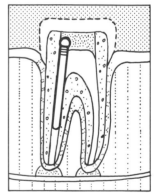

The pulp chamber is sealed and a new crown is placed on the tooth

These drawings demonstrate the progressive treatment of an infected tooth that requires root canal work.

after the operation, as well as the other conditions just described. Indeed, researchers have found that whether a tooth will successfully reattach and actually survive after the operation is related to its condition at the time of the procedure.

Bonding, the Final Restoration

Teeth become discolored for many reasons. Most commonly, these include trauma or the death of a nerve. To correct discoloring, dental professionals bond various materials to tooth surfaces in what has been called the latest in cosmetic dentistry. The procedure is relatively simple. First the unsightly tooth is etched with acid. Afterward, the surface is covered with a tooth-colored material that matches adjoining teeth. The result usually lasts for about five years, and then the bonding must be replaced.

CHAPTER 5

GUM DISEASES

A six-year-old child explores the human mouth at a science museum.

Periodontal, or gum, disease has long plagued humanity. Archaeologists have found signs of it in damaged jawbones of Cro-Magnon man, who lived about 25,000 years ago. And a radiograph of mummified Thuya, mother-in-law of Egyptian Pharaoh Amenhotep III, who lived from 1411–1375 B.C., reveals she had periodontal disease, as well as greatly worn teeth. Pharaoh Merenptah, who lived about 300 years later, had lost all of his back teeth when his gums receded. Moreover, an unidentified lower jaw bone dating from 2900 to 2750 B.C., was found in Egypt with two holes drilled through the bone. Dental experts believe they were made to drain an abscess eroding under a first molar.

Today, the NIDR reports, nearly 80 million Americans are afflicted with *gingivitis,* or inflamed gums, the earliest known form of periodontal disease. This problem has taken the spotlight from tooth decay as the most common dental ailment. According to the NIDR, more than 60% of teeth extracted in the United States are lost because of periodontal disease.

A recent U.S. federal health study found that more than one-third of children aged 6 to 11 and more than two-thirds of adolescents have gingivitis. Yet regardless of a patient's age, the villain of the piece is plaque; the same substance that causes tooth decay also leads to gum disease. Specifically, bacteria in plaque create poisons that irritate gums and can loosen the way gums attach to teeth. Thriving on decaying food, these organisms grow on teeth next to gum edges and cause most types of early periodontal disease.

Gingivitis

Disturbingly, this first stage of periodontal disease has few, if any, symptoms. Gingivitis may even be painless, because it often starts with little more than moderate inflammation, a slight redness and swelling, of gum tissues around the teeth or perhaps some pink on the toothbrush after normal brushing. The inflammation might be due to tartar deposits or bits of food irritating the gums. As the body tries to defend itself from this, it sends a group of red and white blood cells to the area of irritation. Inflammation then occurs and even the slightest touch of a toothbrush might cause the capillaries, or tiny blood vessels nourishing the teeth, to burst. Bleeding gums follow.

Dr. Robert A. Jaffin—the Hackensack, New Jersey, periodontist—has treated gum disease for almost 20 years. He notes, "Periodontal disease is really a bacterial infection, caused by very specific types of bacteria. There are lots of them but basically the biggest group is gram negative aerobes." Some people are not at all susceptible, regardless of the bacteria in their mouths. But, Dr. Jaffin adds, "About 70 to 80 percent of the population will develop periodontal disease that's within the realm of easy treatment. . . . About 15 percent of the population who have a more progressive type of the disease will respond well to treatment, but only if they're diligent and are given proper therapy."

Without treatment, the earlier mild signs become more pronounced. As the disease progresses, bacteria continue accumulating on teeth as well as in the narrow spaces between gum edges and their attachments to teeth. Additional inflammation worsens matters, causing gums to draw back from teeth. Then pockets are formed that can house even more destructive bacteria. The foundation has been laid for the next stage of periodontal disease.

Periodontitis

This second stage, known as *periodontitis,* involves the jawbone together with the gingiva. It has also been called pyorrhea and is considered the most common form of destructive periodontal disease. It is responsible for the loosening of teeth in gums. As the disease advances, plaque hardens into calculus, causing further irritation of the gums, which continue drawing away from the teeth. While detachment of the gums continues, the bones underneath them start to resorb and some teeth will begin to feel loose.

At this point, periodontal pockets may develop. They occur most often between adjacent teeth where toothbrushes cannot reach, occasionally becoming one-half inch deep or more. When inflammation extends along the tooth root, gums begin to turn pale, to dental professionals an obvious symptom of the disease. Bad breath, caused by pus which fills the pockets, is another obvious sign. The gums continue to recede, exposing some of the roots. Ultimately, the connective tissue fibers that fasten teeth to bone are destroyed, and much of the bone socket gradually breaks up. This leads to loosening of the tooth and its gradual loss. As teeth are destroyed, so is supportive bone.

Adult periodontitis, just described, is the most common form of gum disease. In fact, the greatest tooth loss usually does not occur until after age 40. However, localized juvenile periodontitis, or LJP, seen in

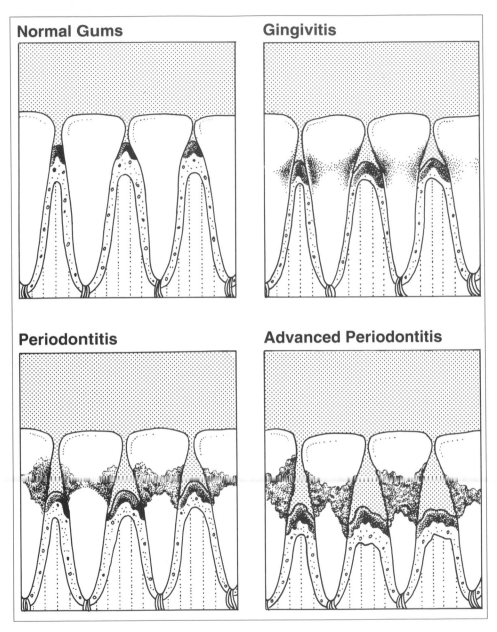

Normal Gums

Gingivitis

Periodontitis

Advanced Periodontitis

Periodontal disease begins whem the gums recede. Not only is gum tissue at risk, but with a greater portion of the tooth exposed, cavities are more likely.

teenagers, is considered a more severe form of the condition. Many dental researchers believe that LJP is caused by a different form of bacteria than the organisms behind the adult form. LJP leads to very rapid tissue destruction but usually affects only the first molars and incisors and perhaps a few additional teeth.

Trench Mouth

Vincent's Infection, more commonly known as "trench mouth," is yet another form of gingivitis. This nickname was coined during World War I because of the prevalence of the condition among soldiers in the European trenches. Modern scientists now think that the condition is caused by a combination of poor nutrition, neglected oral care, and severe stress. Although rarely infectious, trench mouth sometimes occurs in groups of people living closely togther, such as students in dormitories. Most often, these people share similar forms of stress, for example, college mid-term or final examinations.

However, dental experts believe that in most cases this illness is contracted from bacteria that ordinarily live in the mouth. These germs flourish without air, in hard-to-reach areas under tartar and where food is left on teeth or under gum edges. Although they may spread to the rest of the mouth, the bacteria that cause this condition also appear in mouths where there is no sign of the disease. The infection causes painful sores on the gums, making eating difficult. The gums turn bright red at the base, while the small pointed tips that separate teeth become pale and blunt. Moreover, gums bleed when touched, or even on their own. Additional symptoms include an extremely unpleasant odor, pain, and increased saliva flow.

Treatment of Periodontal Disease

Therapies for this disorder can be carried out in a doctor's office or at home, depending on the stage of the disease. In the earliest stages, the simplest treatment consists of scaling or root planing the teeth. The former procedure involves scraping off calculus from the tooth crown

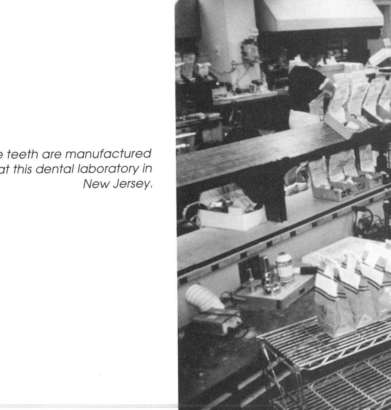

False teeth are manufactured at this dental laboratory in New Jersey.

or root above or beneath the gum line. It is performed by either a dentist or dental hygienist who uses a special sharp instrument to take off the hardened material. Root planing smoothes the root surface to prevent plaque from attaching and to help the gum heal. Scaling is a modern version of what the ancient Greeks and Romans did for cosmetic as well as medical reasons. Celsus and other early practitioners gave detailed advice on following the procedure.

Today, if too much tartar has formed, an additional procedure, called curettage, or "spooning out," is performed. Paired with planing, it removes plaque and infected tissue from the gum pocket walls. If it does not succeed, surgery is usually required to clean out the remaining plaque. About 10 million people undergo this treatment annually.

The newest and most successful treatment for periodontal disease uses chlorhexidine, a topical antibiotic. A topical substance is one that is applied outside the body, like an ointment, instead of being swallowed like a pill. "It's not a true antibiotic," Dr. Jaffin says. "It's an anti-microbial . . . that prevents a dividing of the bacteria. In its highest concentration, it can break down the cells." If periodontal disease does not respond to normal oral hygiene—meticulous brushing and flossing—then chlorhexidine is the treatment of choice, he adds. And the only way that periodontal disease is treated effectively with this substance "is to deliver [it] sub-gingivally," that is, under the gums. This can be achieved with a special attachment to an oral irrigator. It is specially designed to shoot water, mixed with chlorhexidine, at the gums at high pressure in a powerful needlelike spray. "For those who need it," Dr. Jaffin concludes, "it's very, very helpful."

Therapy for trench mouth can be complex. It includes scaling to rid teeth of bacteria. In addition, the doctor may prescribe antibiotics to complete treatment. The medical regimen for trench mouth also calls for dosages of 500 milligrams of vitamin C daily and hourly rinses of a solution of sodium perborate and warm water alternating with a mix of hydrogen peroxide in an equal amount of warm water. Patients are advised to get as much rest as possible and to cease toothbrushing until the specialist feels they have recovered their oral health.

Trench mouth and other gum conditions are irritating and unhealthy. But with systematic care and treatment, they can be eliminated. Perhaps it is even more important to note that, with proper preventative measures, these conditions can be avoided in the first place.

CHAPTER 6

TAKING CARE OF THE TEETH

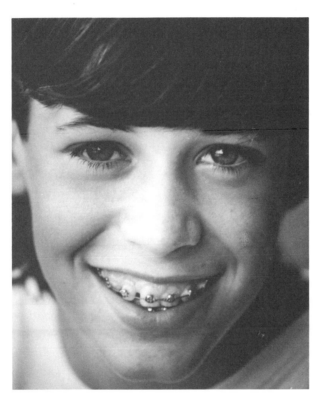

Braces help a person's teeth to grow straight and to form a proper bite.

Most dental problems can be prevented with proper hygiene, diet, oral care, and fluorides. The tradition of good oral hygiene goes back centuries in various cultures. It usually starts with cleanliness. For example, no devout Hindu will eat breakfast without afterwards cleaning teeth, tongue, and mouth. Thus, in India oral hygiene has always included scraping the tongue as well as brushing teeth. In the Western world, Celsus, the physician of ancient Rome, might be considered one of the earliest dental hygienists. He recommended rinsing the mouth with fresh water upon arising from sleep every morning. He also suggested scraping off discoloring stains from teeth, rubbing them with a mixture of pounded rose leaves and various spices, and concluding with a mouth rinse of pure wine.

Later, in seventh-century Arabia, the Koran, Islam's holy book, advised Muslims, adherents of that religion: "You shall clean your teeth for this is a way of praising God," and required rinsing the mouth from 3 to 15 times a day. Early Arabs and Persians cleaned their teeth with pleasantly-flavored sticks. Using one end as a toothpick, they pounded the other end to separate it into a brush. The resulting chew sticks remained popular for many years. Various cleansers were also part of oral hygiene. In Roman times, doctors recommended cleaning teeth with a wide variety of substances, including ground-up cleaned bones and eggshells. The abrasive action of these mixtures, as well as the chalk George Washington used to clean his teeth, resembled that of modern dentifrices.

Toothbrushing

Today, dentists advise that the best way to avoid decay and gum disease is to clean teeth regularly with careful brushing and flossing. Thorough, vigorous toothbrushing should remove plaque from teeth, and the most sensible time to brush is right after eating, before mouth acids have a chance to get started. If a person cannot brush immediately after eating, he or she should do so as soon as possible. It is especially important to brush after dinner, so as to clean the mouth before sleep. As the mouth rests overnight, saliva flow slows down, so this bodily fluid cannot neutralize acid and wash away bacteria as effectively as during the day when it flows in larger amounts. Moreover, when night brushing is skipped, bacteria will have longer to breed on the accumulated food, and the acid they form will stay concentrated until wake-up time.

Correct brushing is not difficult, and if done properly it should not take more than two to four minutes. The experts advise starting with a scrubbing motion on outer tooth surfaces, using gentle strokes and guiding the brush up and down the way that teeth grow. This means moving from the gums down on the upper teeth and from the gums up on the lower teeth. There is a good reason for this: brushing away from the gums prevents brushing food under them. It is also important to force the bristles into spaces between teeth in order to dislodge any bits of trapped food.

Brushing back and forth across most of the teeth, on the other hand, tends to force food into the spaces between them. There is one exception to the up-and-down rule of brushing. The best way to clean flat tooth chewing surfaces is with a scrubbing motion that goes horizontally back to front.

Obviously, teeth cleaning requires effective tools. Most dental professionals recommend choosing a toothbrush with soft, rounded bristle tips and a flat brushing surface for regular use. These tips will not damage gums, and when the brush head is gently rounded there is less chance of injuries to sensitive mouth tissues. The brush itself should be designed to fit far back into the mouth.

One of the smaller models can reach all surfaces of the teeth as well as the gum line. This is important, for brushes are meant to brush and massage gum tissues along with teeth. Equally important, the brush must be in good condition. The rule of thumb is simple. Brushes should be changed every two to three months because by then they will have lost most of their cleaning ability. Electric toothbrushes have become popular over the past few decades. They are small enough to reach into somewhat inaccessible areas and clear away stains and plaque more effectively than hand brushes.

Toothpastes and Fluorides

Whether manual or electric, toothbrushes do not work effectively by themselves. For good oral care, people also need to use dentifrices, substances that help keep the teeth clean and healthy. These include toothpastes, tooth powders, tooth gels, and mouth rinses. In its booklet, *Good Teeth,* the United States Public Health Service sums up what toothpastes and other dentifrices can and cannot do for dental health:

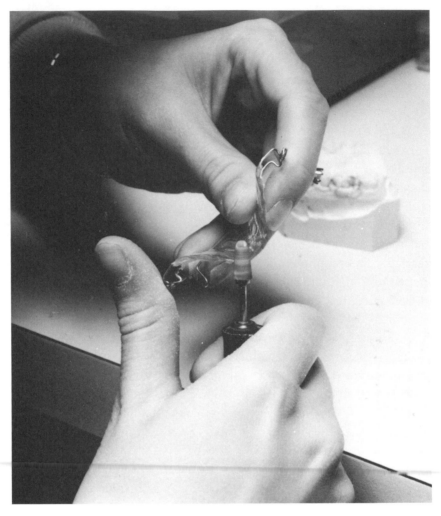

An orthodontist adjusts the shape and fit of a removable brace.

"Tooth pastes and powders are good mechanical aids in cleaning the teeth. To that extent they aid in preventing tooth decay . . . [but they] will not change the color of the teeth, either in one brushing or over a period of time."

In short, dentifrices do not have magical powers. Tartar-control products, toothpastes and rinses alike, do help prevent buildup of tartar, but they only work on new tartar deposits. Once formed, such deposits cannot be loosened by anyone other than a dental professional. On the other hand, certain toothpastes can help prevent decay when they contain fluorides.

In nearly 2,000 U.S. communities, fluorides occur naturally in drinking water. And numerous tests have proven that water containing enough fluoridation can prevent as much as 65% of cavities that might be expected to occur. Just how much is enough? Scientific studies have demonstrated that in order to work effectively against cavities, there should be at least one drop of fluoride in every million drops of water. It does not sound like much, but such a mix produces effective results. A recent ADA report explains: "Fluoride is credited with a dramatic and continuing reduction of children's cavities in the last forty-one years . . . [working] out to a drop in tooth decay of some 36 percent." Part of the explanation for this decrease is that fluorides combine with children's teeth in their formative stages. These are known as systemic, or internal, benefits, because they are absorbed into the body's system. The result is life-long resistance to decay.

Fluorides help protect teeth from decay in at least four ways. First, they strengthen the enamel of developing teeth. Second, they help fully formed teeth resist decay. Acting with minerals in saliva, fluorides restore and harden enamel damaged in the early stages of decay. Finally, because of their presence in saliva, they help cut down the amount of acid produced by bacteria.

People who live where fluoridated water does not occur naturally also have a chance to reap its benefits. Numerous studies have shown that scientists can adjust the amount of fluorides in the water supply safely, effectively, and inexpensively, thereby increasing topical, or external, benefits for teeth already in the mouth. They merely add carefully measured amounts of fluorides to drinking water. This results in better dental health for both children and adults, usually comparable to those who live where fluorides occur naturally in local water supplies. Fluorides can even reverse the formation of microscopic cavities by helping incorporate minerals into teeth, the ADA says. Thus, it recommends using fluoride toothpastes and mouth rinses that it has approved.

A combination of fluoridated water, fluoridated toothpaste, and mouth rinse packs an especially powerful punch against decay. Indeed, scientific studies have shown that people who live in areas with fluoridated water and also use fluoridated toothpaste have lower rates of decay than those who live in the same areas but do not use such dentifrices. Moreover, tooth decay can be effectively prevented in

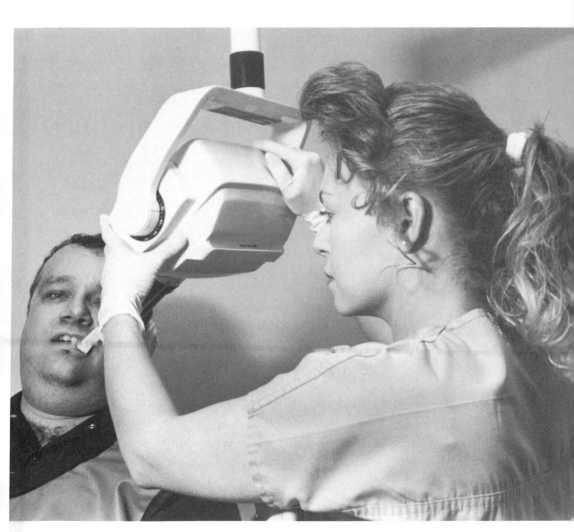

A dental technician prepares to take an X ray.

children who live where fluoridated water is unavailable through the use of fluoride tablets or drops for infants. They provide both topical and systemic benefits. Additional studies have found that when fluoride drops or tablets are consumed from infancy through the teen years, there is 50% to 60% less tooth decay.

Flossing

As an ally in the war against decay, flossing naturally follows toothbrushing. It reaches those spots where brush bristles cannot—between teeth and beneath the gum line. When bits of food linger there, plaque buildup starts.

It takes some practice to floss effectively, but the process is fairly simple. Dentists recommend breaking off about 18 inches of material and wrapping most of it, about 14 inches or so, around the middle finger of one hand. The rest goes around the middle finger of the other hand, to be used for winding up the used floss. Keeping about one inch of material taut between thumbs and forefingers, the floss is gently guided between adjoining teeth until it reaches the gum. Then it is moved away from the gum in a kind of scraping movement along the side of each tooth. This action should be repeated several times before moving on to the next tooth, reeling up the soiled floss as necessary. Users should take special care to floss between the last back teeth and the gums behind them because these spots are often overlooked. At the same time, they must be careful not to let the floss cut gum tissue.

Dental professionals recommend daily flossing, and many would prefer it to follow each meal. If this is not convenient or possible, bedtime is usually best. In any event, they usually advise rinsing the mouth vigorously after the final flossing to flush out bits of debris loosened by this process.

Some patients may find their gums feeling tender after the first few flossings, or even bleeding a little. This is rarely anything to be concerned about because flossing is a form of gum exercise. In fact, if gums hold a lot of plaque when flossing begins, it could take a few days, perhaps even a week, for them to tighten around the teeth again.

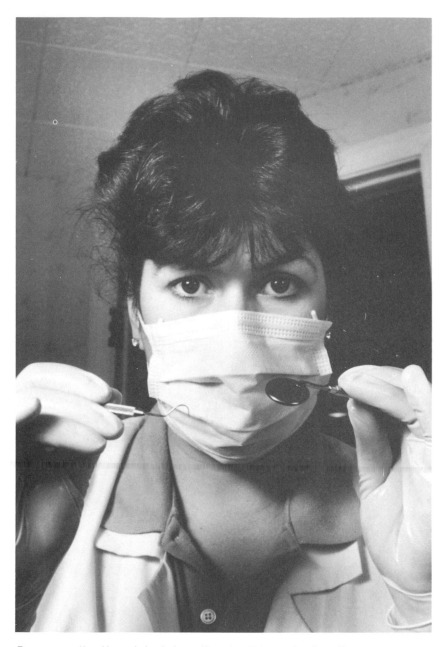

From a patient's point of view, the dentist can look quite intimidating.

However, if a person experiences continued bleeding and soreness, he or she should see a dentist.

Disclosing agents offer another way of checking that brushing and flossing have rid teeth of plaque. These are in the form of tablets that contain a harmless dye. When chewed, they stain teeth a bright red where plaque remains after brushing and flossing. Alternatively, green color can be painted on teeth for the same purpose. In either case, a mirror will reveal the stains. Once identified, remaining plaque can be removed more effectively. These aids to oral health are usually sold in the dental needs area of most drugstores.

Additional Aids to Dental Health

Oral irrigating devices are of two types. Electric models emit pulsating jets of water that cleanse around gums and between teeth where neither brush nor floss can reach. Nonelectric models attach to a faucet and proceed in the same way. Most dental professionals suggest the first type because patients can regulate water pressure and temperature most easily with it. Although these devices are not recommended for small children, they are considered especially helpful for anyone over 12 years of age, particularly those wearing *orthodontic bands*. When the water stream is aimed at them, it flushes out food particles otherwise untouched.

Basically, irrigators consist of a container that holds water, plus a small tube or hose. The container is filled with lukewarm water, and the hose's tip is pointed at the gumline. After the user adjusts the device to the desired pressure, he or she turns it on and directs jets of water at both the inside and outside gum surfaces. When used properly, this device flushes out a surprising amount of debris as well as bacteria.

Experts feel that irrigators should be used at least once a day, especially for patients with orthodontic bands or gum problems. When someone does not have these special needs, four or five irrigations a week should suffice. But dentists warn that this treatment is no substitute for careful brushing and flossing because it does not remove plaque.

Tooth Sealants

Yet another weapon in the war against decay in children's teeth is the tooth sealant. The ADA considers it vital for reducing cavities in permanent teeth as they erupt, starting around the age of six. Dentists are especially concerned with children's back teeth, which have long been prone to cavities, in spite of help from fluorides. In fact, according to Dr. Leonard A. Cohen, chairman of the University of Maryland's Department of Oral-Care Delivery in Baltimore, "Sealants take up where fluorides leave off." When they are teamed with fluoridated water and such topical fluorides as toothpastes, mouth rinses, and fluoride gel, they "virtually eliminate decay," he added.

Sealants are clear or shaded plastic resins that dental professionals apply to the biting surfaces of molars. Such substances work by filling in the minute pits and fissures where food gets easily caught. In this way, they protect tooth enamel from plaque and decay-causing acids that cannot penetrate the plastic film. In fact, small cavities caught under the sealant do not grow but actually tend to remineralize or reform the enamel.

Applying a sealant is a fast and painless procedure. First, the dentist cleans each tooth that will be sealed, then etches it with a mild acid wash to roughen the surface to which the sealant will cling. Next, a plastic coating is painted on and dried. This guarantees that the back teeth will not develop cavities for at least two years, although the plastic coating can last for up to five years. Even so, the ADA suggests that sealants be checked during regular dental visits to see whether reapplication is needed. Recent studies sponsored by the association report that children whose teeth were treated with sealants had a 6% cavity rate of back teeth as opposed to a 59% rate without sealants.

Dental Prophylaxis

It is everyone's responsibility to brush and floss properly. It is also the dentist's or dental hygienist's responsibility to clean patients' teeth regularly during a procedure called dental prophylaxis. This is a three-step process. First, surface deposits are removed, taking off calculus and softer deposits from around exposed bone. Once tooth surfaces are cleaned, the polishing phase begins. Second, a special kind of toothpaste is applied to the teeth, followed by careful flossing between them. Finally, if topical fluoride was erased during the first two steps, it is now replaced.

Diet and Nutrition

Proper nutrition is the foundation of good oral health. It starts with an expectant mother's diet and continues through children's growing years, into adolescence and young adulthood, and beyond.

What the expectant mother eats affects her baby's health, especially its developing teeth. She needs foods rich in protein, plus the important vitamins A, C, and D, together with the minerals calcium and phosphorus. Calcium is important for the cells that help harden facial bones and jawbones, but this mineral needs vitamins A, C, and D for proper calcification. All of these nutrients pass through the umbilical cord to be absorbed by the baby's growing skeleton and tooth buds. So the expectant mother must eat sensibly, because following a balanced diet will help keep her own teeth healthy as the baby develops a healthy set of its own.

The mother's daily regimen should include a large glass of citrus fruit juice, fresh fruit, whole-grain breads and cereals, and three to four glasses of milk. She may get protein from eggs, lean meats, poultry, fish, cheese, or the combination of beans and grains that form a complete protein. Eating sensibly is the first step towards a balanced diet, which is built around items chosen from the four basic food groups: milk and dairy products, fruits and vegetables, grain products such as bread and cereals, and proteins.

Where tooth decay is concerned, the main culprits are refined sugars and starches. Refined foods have been changed from their natural state by specific production processes. This leads to the loss of their natural vitamins, minerals, and other nutritional values. Refined foods are usually very soft and stick to the teeth, leaving them vulnerable to tooth decay. Candy, pastry, jelly, and other sweets use refined sugars. White bread, polished white rice, and various types of dry cereals are, or contain, refined starches. Once these foods enter a person's mouth they form the acids described earlier.

By contrast, foods made with whole meal, whole rye, whole grain oats, brown rice, and their assorted by-products are doubly helpful. These are not only more nutritious but also more fibrous, or coarse. This coarseness keeps them from sticking to the teeth the way refined sugars and starches do. By not sticking there is a smaller chance that the acids which cause decay will form. Americans and the British eat more refined foods than any other people in the world, which at least partially explains why they have more cavities than any other people.

Although no health professional would ever suggest eating sugar, it helps to know that *when* sugar is eaten is more important than *how much* is eaten. Eating sugary food at mealtimes is far less harmful to teeth than doing so throughout the day. The equivalent of 20 teaspoonfuls of sugar taken in one meal is far less damaging to teeth than 5 teaspoonfuls eaten throughout the day in snacks. This is because the first instance causes only a single acid attack; the second example causes five separate ones. Many studies have shown that saliva is a natural neutralizer of the acids that result from eating and drinking sugary foods and drinks. So if someone nibbles on sweets and drinks sugary sodas often between meals, there will not be sufficient saliva to neutralize the great amount of dangerous acid on the teeth. That is why dental professionals and dieticians advise serving sweets, if they are served at all, immediately at the end of meals, when saliva can help fight the acid buildup.

CHAPTER 7

ORTHODONTICS

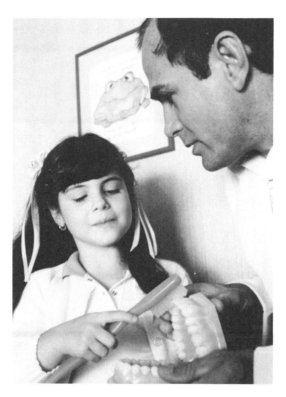

A dentist uses an enlarged model to teach young patients how to brush their teeth.

The term *orthodontics* comes from two Greek words: *ortho,* meaning straight, and *odons,* meaning tooth. An orthodontist uses specific appliances to move teeth into their correct positions and to ensure that they remain that way. This dental specialist wants to give the patient a good bite, well-functioning, healthy teeth, and a better appearance. The cosmetic effect is important because looking as attractive as possible helps build self-esteem. A good bite also eases the strain on jaw joints and muscles that occurs when teeth do not meet correctly. Straight teeth help keep gums and other oral tissues in good condition, reducing the possibility of gingival disease. It is also easier to keep them clean through brushing and flossing, because they are less apt to catch and hold food that could cause decay.

Some estimates claim that from 50% to 90% of American children between the ages of 12 and 17 require orthodontic treatment. That is, their teeth need some kind of improved alignment or *spacing*. Other studies report that one out of five school-age children have severe orthodontic problems, especially variations of malocclusion. These problems involve function as well as appearance.

Judging the Need for Orthodontic Treatment

During children's growing years, from early childhood through late adolescence, their jaws develop constantly. They change from the doll-like features of babies to the mature appearance of young adults. At various stages through that period, depending upon the kind of orthodontic need, the specialist harnesses this growth to guide crooked or otherwise misplaced teeth into their normal relationships.

Starting with the earliest years, parents can often judge whether their offspring will need orthodontic treatment. Some obvious signs are a child, eight years old, or older, who has irregular front teeth that are turned in, out, or set sideways; obvious spaces between front teeth; an open space between top and bottom front teeth occurring when the back teeth are touching; speech problems; biting the cheek or the roof of the mouth; and grinding or clenching the teeth.

Few people have a perfect bite. Occasionally they have a single tooth or even several teeth that are not properly aligned. In other cases, severe abnormalities can cause distortion of the entire face. All of these are examples of malocclusion, or imperfect bite. When a bite is only slightly off, the teeth function well and look relatively straight. But a more pronounced defect requires orthodontic correction, for poor bite can cause deformities of the face and jaws. It can also place additional strain on gums and facial bones, leading eventually to periodontal disease.

Malocclusion falls into several categories. In class I, the teeth are set too far apart or are crowded or crooked. Buck teeth, sometimes called *overbite,* along with teeth set in a receding jaw, referred to as a weak chin, fall into class II. Class III includes bulldog jaw, or prognathism, which has the lower jaw biting too far front and the upper biting too far back. Various orthodontic problems do not fall into these categories. One example is when molars meet while incisors remain open, leading to *open bite.* If not corrected this, too, can cause periodontal disease. Another example is when the upper teeth bite down and cover the lower ones, making chewing uncomfortable.

What causes malocclusion? Occasionally, poor bite is congenital. A child might inherit from one parent a jaw too small to hold the large teeth inherited from the other parent. More often, though, it is caused by any of several factors. For example, acquired malocclusion can stem from such poor oral habits as thumb sucking. If this practice continues past the age of about 18 months and into early childhood, it can affect a child's bite. Depending upon how intensively the thumb is sucked and for how long, the upper jaw and teeth will eventually be pulled too far forward for a good bite. Such malocclusion results from the abnormal pressure this practice places on front teeth, pushing them out of alignment, while the other teeth react by drifting out of position.

A bad bite can also be due to poor timing. On occasion, a primary tooth does not fall out naturally when a permanent one is ready to erupt into the jaw to replace it. In this situation the second tooth erupts in an irregular position while the primary one stays put. Until normal eruption occurs, there is malocclusion among the remaining teeth.

Treatment of Malocclusion

In very young children, preventative orthodontics might precede full appliances, popularly known as braces. In fact, such early treatment could move jaw bones and chewing muscles into the right positions,

One of the most overlooked but effective methods of preventing tooth decay is proper nutrition begun at an early age.

preparing the mouth for stability of bite and offering the best possible correction at an early age. One example of preventive treatment involves extraction of a primary tooth prior to the eruption of its replacement. Otherwise, the first tooth could hold back the permanent one. Meanwhile, a brace called a space retainer holds that gap open, keeping neighboring teeth from tipping into the empty space until the permanent tooth is ready to fill it. The retainer resembles a pair of metal bands that are attached to adjoining teeth to bridge the gap.

Occasionally, interceptive orthodontics is used when a jaw is too small to hold permanent teeth without crowding. For instance, the specialist might remove permanent premolars starting to erupt when a patient is nine-and-a-half years old. The extraction makes space for permanent canines to emerge. Afterward, the mouth will lack four premolars but contain a number of straight, uncrowded teeth that mesh with their opposites. Interceptive orthodontics might be called on even earlier. For example, when thumb sucking is a problem an orthodontist will prescribe a habit corrector to prevent the malocclusion that this particular habit causes. It is also used to prevent tongue thrusting, or pushing the tongue against the teeth when swallowing, which could have a similar effect. All bad oral habits must be corrected before orthodontic treatment can begin.

If the specialist decides against interceptive orthodontics, he or she usually follows a standard procedure. It starts with an evaluation of the structure and condition of the patient's mouth, which includes careful examination of teeth, jaws, jaw joints, face, and profile. Next, a series of X rays is taken. The doctor goes over them with precise measurements that show just how the patient's bite can be corrected. Models of the bite follow. These are made of plaster of paris molded over jaw impressions. The molds show how teeth and jaws fit together, helping in the preparation of the final appliances used to straighten teeth and correct the bite.

Orthodontic Appliances

Preteens and teenagers are most apt to undergo orthodontic treatment because their permanent teeth are in and their jaws have matured. Braces are usually associated with this process. Working with wires and various attachments, specialists apply gentle pressure to push teeth and jaws into proper alignment. That pressure causes specific parts of the jawbone to dissolve. Yet the tooth movement is so gentle that new bone has a chance to fill in around it. When the jawbone can support a tooth in its new position, the braces may be removed.

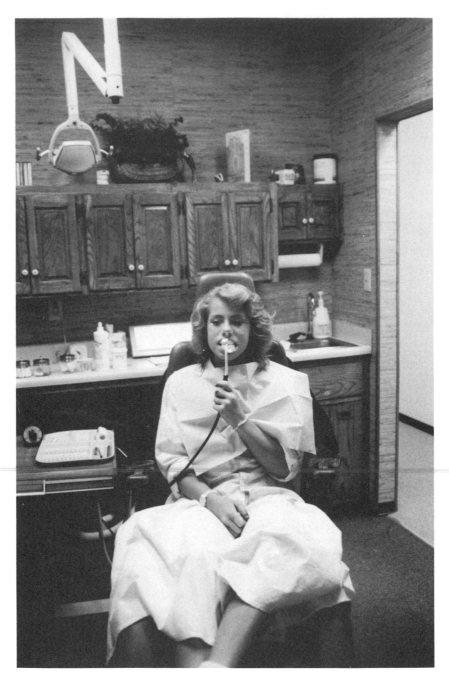

A patient gives herself a fluoride treatment.

There are many kinds of orthopedic devices. Some of them, such as those called brackets, are considered universal by specialists because they will accommodate most patients. They come in square or rectangular shapes and, made of ceramic or metal, attach to an orthodontic band. But brackets can also be bonded directly to teeth with acid-etched materials, thereby eliminating the need for bands. Major aids in the orthodontic process, brackets hold strong, fine wire set on the inside or outside of each tooth. In turn, the wire exerts a steady force on the dental arch. When the doctor makes special bends in the brackets they also open or close spaces or move teeth.

Conversely, those bands—best known as braces—are custom-fitted to meet individual needs. Circular stainless steel appliances, the bands are normally cemented around each tooth and sometimes hold hooks to which elastics, or rubber bands, are attached. Essential to orthodontic treatment, the elastics supply the pressure needed to position teeth and jaws correctly. This means that they must be placed and used precisely as the orthodontist directs. The elastics may stretch from the upper to the lower teeth in various ways, depending upon the patient's bite problem.

As patients start wearing braces they may experience some discomfort. It could be a sense of tenderness in the teeth or even a feeling that they are slightly loose. This feeling will probably return whenever the appliances are adjusted. But it does not last throughout the entire course of treatment.

Eventually, when the teeth have moved into their correct positions, the appliances are removed, and any remaining cement is cleaned from the teeth. More often than not, patients may wear a retaining appliance, which keeps teeth in their newly corrected positions until new bone has filled in around the roots. A retainer may be worn for a year or more. It may be fixed or removed by the patient during meals and oral care. The doctor determines when it is safe to remove retainers.

Dollars and Cents, Weeks and Months

What will orthodontic treatment cost? How long does it take to achieve satisfactory results? Generally speaking, overall costs of orthodontics vary according to the nature of the problems being corrected. When they are mild, costs will be lower than for correction of severe malocclusion.

Dr. Robert Bray is an orthodontist who practices in the Atlantic City, New Jersey, area. A spokesperson for the Northeast Chapter of the American Academy of Orthodontists, he reports costs of about $3,200 for conventional treatment of children, that is, the use of braces. This covers a period of 20 to 24 months of therapy and one year of retention. Adult costs are somewhat higher, from $3,500 to $3,800.

Different materials may be used for these services, with costs rising accordingly. For instance, if acrylic brackets are used instead of metal ones, the fee can increase by $250 for each jaw. However, for many older patients it is worth the extra fee because these appliances are less noticeable. Some brackets are called "invisible." Usually used to treat adults, they are placed on the back side of teeth. This raises the cost from $6,400 to $6,800. The price is greater because, unlike the "universal" brackets, these have to be made individually from impressions of each tooth.

Early correction of what might become oral problems can involve different costs. For example, if the family dentist feels a child is developing an overbite, he or she might refer the patient to a specialist for the preventative treatment mentioned earlier. According to Dr. Bray, this early "guiding treatment" can cost from $1,550 to $1,850 for a treatment period of 12 to 18 months. The patient is examined at regular intervals afterward, so that the orthodontist and family dentist can judge if, or when, the patient is ready for braces. Should a decision be made to have the treatment, Dr. Bray's office, like many others, will subtract the guidance fee from a full conventional charge. In addition, there may be partial fees for various incidental items, for example, a habit corrector. These can run from $450 to $650. With luck, they will make a complete, more expensive course of treatment unnecessary.

Surgical Correction of Malocclusion

Orthodontics helps change the position of the teeth to improve their health and appearance. But it cannot correct malformation of facial

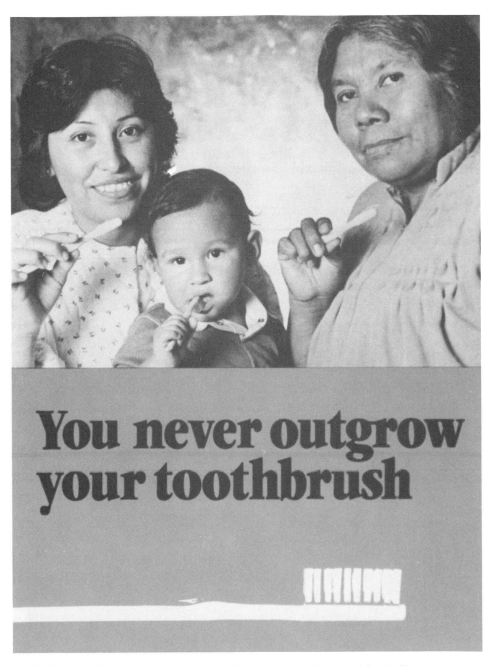

Public information campaigns stress that preventative brushing is the best defense against dental problems.

bones, often called skeletal irregularities. This requires surgery, which is usually performed in a hospital. Surgery can correct facial deformities relating to both teeth and jaws. For instance, a mandible could be moved backward or the maxilla moved forward by cutting and repositioning the bone. For best results, orthodontists and oral surgeons coordinate their treatment on this type of malocclusion. As one example, Dr. Bray might delay some orthodontic work until a patient has recovered from surgery that repositioned the jaws. Or he would do some repositioning before the surgery and continue his work after its completion.

CHAPTER 8

LOOKING AHEAD

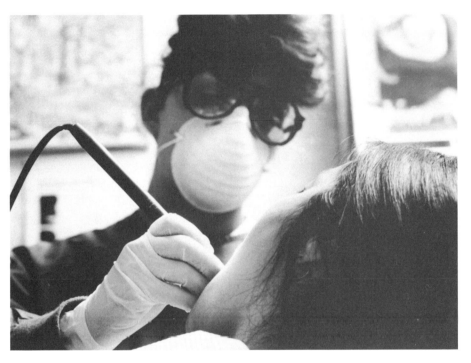

A dental hygienist uses an ultrasonic tool to clean a patient's teeth.

Through advances in science and technology, dentistry has undergone an enormous shift in emphasis. It has moved from correction of existing problems to far-reaching research projects that include disease prevention. For instance, dental scientists are now focusing on less painful therapies for periodontal disease, including the use of lasers. And under the auspices of the NIDR, experiments continue toward preventing plaque and decay from forming by using special antiseptic mouthwashes.

Farewell Decay?

According to the NIDR, an antidecay vaccine could reach dental offices toward the end of the century. Moreover, experiments with weak electric current have pushed fluoride ions, or electrically charged molecules, deep into a tooth's dentin, possibly leading to even greater protection against decay in that vulnerable area. Soon, scientists may insert genetically altered material into a tooth to help it repair damaged enamel.

For many years there were few techniques that could identify decay-prone people—those whom dental researchers label "high risk." Now, however, NIDR investigators have created improved sampling techniques to spot causes of decay in such patients. These could be specific organisms or molecules. Success would mean safe, accurate methods for identifying decay-prone children. Eventually, it may be possible to cut down risk conditions for these youngsters and preserve their teeth.

Dentists know that the bacterium *Streptococcus mutans* causes tooth decay through the colonies it builds in the mouth. But scientists at the Forsyth Dental Center in Boston discovered a mutant, or changed, strain, which they named JH105. It also colonizes but is not harmful, generating too little acid to cause cavities. Developed in the laboratory, it is capable of colonizing the mouth, while producing a substance that is lethal to *Streptococcus mutans* but harmless to other oral bacteria. The effects JH105 has on the original bacteria have led researchers to call this "a major step toward the elimination of dental decay." It is simply a matter of replacement therapy. In other words, the new, harmless, or innocuous strain will be substituted for the harmful bacteria that stick to teeth and produce large amounts of decay-causing acids.

On the same front, NIDR-supported researchers have developed a device that holds a long-lasting fluoride pellet. When attached to a back tooth, it bathes the mouth with a low but continuous dose of the substance. A dentist would change the pellet periodically. About five years away from approval, it promises to be especially helpful for the decay-prone.

Saving Time and Money

Thanks to dentists from several European countries, computers have become major dental aids. In France, Switzerland, and elsewhere on the European continent, dental practitioners now use a computer system called Computer Aided Design/Computer Aided Manufacturing, or CAD/CAM, for swift prosthodontic treatment. With CAD/CAM, they can fit patients with dental crowns, bridges, and other restorations in a single visit. For a crown, the tooth is prepared in the usual way. But instead of making an impression to be sent to a dental lab, the practitioner uses a sophisticated imaging device, or probe, that reads, or maps, the tooth's contours. It produces a computer-generated three-dimensional copy that may be studied from every angle. The image then goes to a high-precision milling machine that uses various cutting tools to carve out the crown. Not long afterward, it is permanently installed in the patient's mouth. Considering how much time it takes to make a standard crown or denture, it is easy to see why this new procedure has been labeled as revolutionary.

And this is not the last word on CAD/CAM technology. At the University of Alabama, Tuscaloosa, a system is being developed to pick up further detail on the tooth. Researchers, led by Reggie Caudhill, professor of engineering, are working on a spray for the tooth surface to help the computer picture it more fully. He predicts that American consumers will soon see CAD/CAM technology in their dentists' offices.

Moreover, CAD/CAM can be used for cosmetic surgery. The North Suburban Dental Association, founded by Dr. Barry Freydberg in

Skokie, Illinois, consists of 12 dental practitioners with many specialties. Even so, about 30% of their patient load comes for cosmetic dentistry. It is a "computer-friendly practice," Dr. Freydberg says. With a computer, plus a dental imaging software package, technicians can show patients a computerized image of how they will look after cosmetic oral-dental surgery.

It is important to develop a good relationship with your dentist and, as with any medical procedure, to demand a full explanation of the work to be performed.

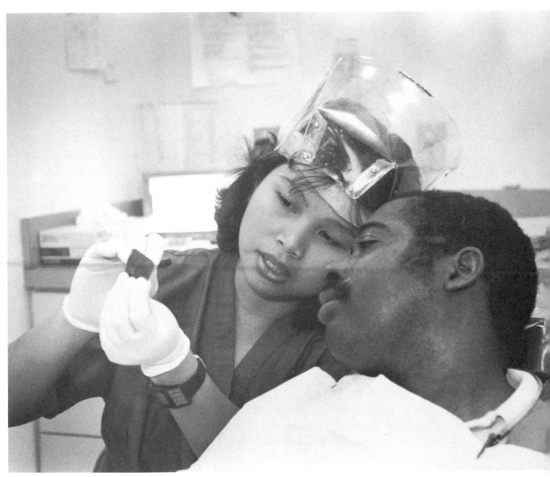

Good News in Orthodontics

According to a recent article in the *Journal of the American Dental Association,* or *JADA,* ongoing research at the University of Pennsylvania School of Dental Medicine should lead to reduced treatment time for patients. Started in 1982, the research centered on a nickel-sized device that delivers a small electric current to the gum tissues. According to the article, "Miniature battery paddles attached to the teeth by orthodontic appliances are worn inside the mouth to deliver a constant current into the gums, one too small to be felt." Researchers believe that this direct current "stimulates specialized tooth-supporting bone tissue cells that break down and build up bone." As cells respond increasingly, there is a speedup of the "desired re-arrangement of bone tissues" that support the tooth's root. Human clinical trials, begun in 1986, have shown favorable results. This means faster orthodontic tooth movement and reduced treatment time in the foreseeable future.

Sealants for Adults

JADA has also reported on a new technology being developed to protect dental patients of all ages against tooth decay. Researchers are studying materials and techniques that would provide a very thin coating over the entire crown and root surfaces of teeth and thus protect them from decay-causing bacteria. The coating would still be transparent and colorless, "or pigmented to hide discolored tooth enamel," the report said.

This improvement on the sealants described earlier "will have great potential for preventing root caries in adults." Specifically, according to Dr. Rafael Bowen, now director of the ADA Health Foundation, Paffenberger Research Center, that means a growing percentage of the dental population. When people age, their gums recede, exposing more of the tooth root surface. Decay increases in the root because the surface is softer and more susceptible to decay than tooth crowns. As a preventative measure, this new coating stays in place, providing a physical barrier between the tooth surface and its surrounding oral environment, which is filled with colonies of destructive bacteria.

When perfected, the coating would block them and thus prevent the production of decay-causing acids.

Improved Tooth Restoration

In March 1991, *JADA* reported on the introducton of "preformed, tooth-colored glass-ceramic inserts" for three classes of cavities. Researchers anticipate such improvements as "increased stiffness and durability of the composite . . . and additional . . . stability of the remaining tooth crown during hardening." Extensive clinical trials continued, and the new technology reached dentist's offices by 1993. Marketing started with kits of inserts containing three or four standardized shapes in "the most utilized tooth shades." In time, more shades, shapes, and sizes will be added.

New Enzymes and Plastics

In 1991, dental researchers reported that new high-tech methods for diagnosing periodontitis would soon be commercially available to periodontists. They include new materials for biochemical analysis of enzymes in gingival crevicular fluid, the liquid found in the crevices between gums, said Dr. Roy C. Page of the University of Washington. Those enzymes, including interleukin-1 and prostaglandin E2, are often present when the disease is active in teeth-supporting bone. "Other enzymes, such as collagenase, are now known to destroy the connective gum tissue," Dr. Page added.

These new diagnostic methods are also being combined with such other high-tech tools as color-coded digital radiography, which is a new type of computerized X ray. Marjorie Jeffcoat, of the University of Alabama, Birmingham, explained that on separate visits the dentist takes two of these special X rays, then compares the images on a computer. He or she can detect any difference, as little as 0.1 mm of bone change around teeth and dental implants, and go on to uncover progressive periodontal disease with over 90% accuracy. Changes are much harder to detect on conventional X rays. Dr. Jeffcoat also de-

Though new dental technologies are continually being developed in the Industrialized world where many people have the money to pay for them, in Third World countries there is an urgent need for more dentists, more basic dental services, and education to prevent tooth decay.

scribed electronic probing, another computerized method that can detect less than 0.4 mm of soft tissue loss, thus indicating the earliest stages of periodontal disease.

In addition, scientists are currently working on the development of new restorative materials and techniques. When they succeed, dentists will be able to repair decayed teeth with a minimum of drilling. Also, there will be less removal of healthy tooth structure than is normally required for traditional restoration. Moreover, the NIDR has perfected techniques that have doubled and tripled the strength of the bonds between the synthetics and dentin.

The institute is also pioneering in research that has discovered some superior restorative materials for fillings. Dental practitioners who have used these latest plastics—called light-cured resins—say that they adhere to teeth more securely than other materials. They also look better and make teeth less sensitive to extremes of temperature. And the new plastics are easier to use, providing a double savings for patients: less time for treatment plus reduced costs.

Painless Dentistry

There are some 500 dentists around the world who use laser technology mainly to treat gum disease. Indeed, the U.S. Food and Drug Administration has approved this procedure for the treatment of soft tissue, such as the cutting and trimming of gums. The dental laser is a low-power laser, using about 3 watts, as compared with the 100-watt laser used in welding. It produces a beam of pulsating, concentrated light that can vaporize specific cells of diseased skin without damaging neighboring, healthy tissues. In dentistry, the laser treats gum disease by killing bacteria between teeth and gums, then vaporizing unwanted tissue, together with the tartar that helps bacteria adhere to teeth. At 150 pulses per second, each beam numbs the affected area yet is too rapid to send a message of pain from the nerves to the brain. So patients feel relatively little discomfort. In addition, the beam seals off blood vessels, sterilizing the area while cutting down on the danger of infection. And the entire procedure can be carried out without needles or anesthesia.

Lasers operate on the principle that dark, diseased tissues absorb light faster than do light, healthy tissues. According to Dr. Eugene Seidner, of Caldwell, New Jersey, because a dental laser operates on such a low power, "If you slip, you can't cut anybody's tongue or lip off." Understandably, he calls this therapy "very good, very precise." None of the patients whom Dr. Seidner treated in one three-month period in 1991 needed Novocain, he reports. "There was no pain, or only tolerable pain." So the laser has "tremendous value" for children, as well as for senior citizens who are already using medication, pregnant women, and anyone else who should avoid anesthesia. Lasers "haven't replaced" such conventional instruments as high-speed drills for cavities inside the tooth, Dr. Seidner concludes, but when the laser can be used, it means more comfort for the patient.

Dental Offices Move Toward the 21st Century

Some practitioners and researchers refer to modern dental offices and their equipment as space age dentistry. For instance, drills have been updated so that many current models run at 500,000 revolutions per minute without vibration. They can cut a tooth like butter and fully prepare a small cavity in a couple of minutes. Some have fiber-optic light attachments, giving the dentist intensified light for improved vision within the mouth.

Ultrasonics, or the medical use of sound waves, has also emerged onto today's dental scene. One such high-speed tool scales teeth, while another—an ultrasonic kit—helps the dentist cut a gum without pain or bleeding, making it somewhat akin to laser treatment.

In the 21st century, most people may reasonably anticipate better oral health. Because of current research projects, they can look forward to the eradication of decay, the conquest of periodontal disease, and improved facial appearance through advances in orthodontic therapy. Once scientists achieve these breakthroughs, the rest depends upon how people care for their teeth and mouths. A person's slogan should be: Brush and floss carefully and faithfully, eat nutritiously and avoid foods that undermine dental and oral health, and use fluoridated toothpaste and other tooth products. And, of course, get regular dental checkups and follow the advice of dental professionals. The result should be improved dental health and smiles.

APPENDIX:
FOR MORE INFORMATION

The following is a list of organizations that can provide further information on the issues discussed in this book.

GENERAL INFORMATION

American Dental Association
211 East Chicago Avenue
Chicago, IL 60611
(312) 440-2500

American Dental Hygienists Association
444 North Michigan Avenue, Suite 3400
Chicago, IL 60611
(800) 243-2342

National Institute of Dental Research
9000 Rockville Pike
Bethesda, MD 20892
(301) 496-2351

ORTHODONTICS

American Association of Orthodontists
401 North Lindbergh Boulevard
St. Louis, MO 63141-7816
(314) 993-1700

FURTHER READING

American Dental Association. *Tooth Survival Book*. Chicago: American Dental Association, 1977.

Ash, Major M., Jr. *Wheeler's Atlas of Tooth Form*. 5th ed. Philadelphia: Saunders, 1988.

Berland, Theodore, and Alfred Seyler. *Your Children's Teeth: A Complete Guide for Parents*. New York: Meredith Press, 1968.

Besford, John. *Good Mouthkeeping, or How To Save Your Children's Teeth and Your Own While You're at It*. 2nd ed. New York: Oxford University Press, 1984.

Collins, Daniel A. *Your Teeth: A Handbook of Dental Care for the Whole Family*. Garden City, NY: Doubleday, 1967.

Cranin, A. Norman. *The Modern Family Guide to Dental Health*. New York: Stein and Day, 1971.

Ehrlich, Ann. *Nutrition and Dental Health: A Teacher's Manual*. Albany, NY: Delmar, 1987.

Hoffman-Axtheim, Walter A. *History of Dentistry*. Chicago: Quintessence, 1981.

Katz, Simon. *Preventive Dentistry in Action*. Upper Montclair, NJ: D.C.P., 1981.

Kendall, Bonnie. *Opportunities in Dental Care Careers.* Lincolnwood, IL: V.G.M. Career Horizons, 1990.

Langlais, Robert, and Craig S. Miller. *Color Atlas of Common Oral Diseases.* Malvern, PA: Lea Febiger, 1990.

Lantner, Minna, and Gerald Bender. *Understanding Dentistry.* Boston: Boston Press, 1969.

McGuire, Thomas. *The Tooth Trip.* New York: Random House, 1979.

Marshall, Howard B. *How To Save Your Teeth: The Preventive Approach.* New York: Penguin, Everest House, 1980.

Massler, Maury, and Isaac Schour. *Atlas of the Mouth.* 2nd ed. Chicago: American Dental Association, 1981.

National Institute for Dental Research. *Broadening the Scope: Long-Range Research Plan for the Nineties.* NIH Publication Number 901188. September 1990.

Nourse, Alan. *The Tooth Book.* New York: McKay, 1977.

Nyugen, Thanh, and Patty de Rouff. *Your Mouth—Oral Care for All Ages.* Radnor, PA: Chilton Book, 1979.

Renner, Robert. *An Introduction to Dental Anatomy.* Chicago: Quintessence, 1985.

Ring, Malvin E. *Dentistry—An Illustrated History.* New York: Harry N. Abrams: 1985.

Tainter, Jerry, and Mary Jane Tainter. *The Oral Report—The Consumer's Common Sense Guide to Better Dental Care.* New York: Facts on File, 1988.

GLOSSARY

abscess an infection in the tooth pulp

alveolar process the part of the jawbone where the roots of the teeth are embedded

apex the tip of the tooth's root

caries tooth decay

cavity a hole in a tooth caused by decay

crown the part of the tooth that shows above the gum line, or an artificial substitute

cusp a pointed projection that is part of the tooth's chewing or biting surface

dental arch the upper or lower dental ridge in the jawbone, with or without teeth

dentin the substance that forms the bulk of a tooth under the enamel

denture a removable or fixed plasticlike appliance that replaces all or part of missing teeth

disclosing agent a chemical solution that stains plaque on teeth to make it visible and therefore easily removed

extraction the removal of all or part of a tooth

filling the material used to restore part of a tooth that has decayed

gingiva the technical term for the gum

gingivitis an inflamation of the gum tissue; the start of periodontal disease

impacted tooth a tooth caught in the jawbone in such a way that it will never erupt

malocclusion a condition in which upper and lower teeth do not mesh together properly, causing a poor bite

mandible the technical term for the lower jaw

maxilla the technical term for the upper jaw

occlusion popularly known as the bite; technically, the relation of the upper and lower teeth and jaws

open bite a bite in which the teeth do not meet properly; usually requires orthodontic treatment

orthodontic band a stainless steel appliance cemented around a tooth with brackets that hold orthodontic wires and elastics

orthodontics a dental specialty that is concerned with correcting crooked teeth and, in so doing, producing a better bite

overbite a kind of malocclusion—in this case a vertical or horizontal over-lap—that requires orthodontic treatment

periodontal a term referring to the gums and underlying bone

periodontal ligament strong fibers that attach a tooth to the supporting jawbone

periodontitis an advanced stage of gum disease

plaque a sticky deposit of material that looks like gelatin and clings to a tooth's surface; bacteria that form in plaque cause tooth decay and gum disease

pontics tooth replacement in a dental bridge, usually soldered to crowns placed on neighboring teeth

pulp soft, living tissue in the center of a tooth that forms dentin and maintains the life of the tooth

pulp chamber the space in a tooth's center that is surrounded by dentin and holds the dental pulp

resorption the physiological dissolution of a tooth or bone structure

restoration any kind of filling that replaces the part of a tooth destroyed by decay

root the portion of the tooth under the crown that extends into the jawbone; it is hollow, and holds pulp tissue that is removed during root canal therapy

root canal the space in the root that holds pulp tissue

root canal therapy the process of removing pulp from the root canal; cleaning, shaping, and sterilizing it; and then filling the canal

saliva ejector a device that removes saliva and water from the mouth during dental treatment

spacing a gap between teeth

wisdom tooth a third molar

INDEX

Abscess, 38, 55, 62

Acid, 23, 37, 60, 73, 78, 80, 92
   lactic, 36
   organic, 36
   wash, 78

Albucasis, 14, 55

Allogenic transplant, 58

Alveolar bone, 21

Alveolar process, 21

Alveolus, 20

Ameloblasts, 17

American Dental Association (ADA), 46,
   73, 78

Anesthesia, 42, 46, 47, 55, 98, 99
   liquid, 48

Antibiotics, 39

Antidecay vaccine, 92

Articulator, 51

Autogenic transplant, 58

Autogenous graft operations, 44

Baby teeth, 17, 28. *See also* Teeth: primary

Bacteria, 36, 37, 53, 62, 63, 65, 68, 70, 73,
   77, 92, 95, 98

Barber-surgeons, 14

Berman, Charles, 57

Bicuspids, 19, 26, 53

Bite, 83, 84, 85

Bite impression, 50

Black, C. V., 46

Bonding, 60

Bone
   autogenous, 42
   bank, 44
   grafts, 42
   infection, 40

Borden Dental Laboratories, 51

Braces, 83, 84, 85, 88

Bridges, 52, 53, 93

Buck teeth, 83. *See also* Overbite

Bulldog jaw, 83

Burs, 14, 46.

Calcification, 23, 79

Calcium, 17, 23, 79
   salts, 36

Calculus, 37, 63, 65, 79. *See also* Tartar

Canine teeth, 18, 20, 32, 85. *See also*
   Cuspids

Cap. *See* Crown: artificial

Carbon-free phosphate, 51

Cavities, 38, 45, 73, 78, 80, 92, 99
   deep, 38, 53
   and diet, 80
   prevention of, 73, 78

Celsus, 13, 37, 66, 70

Cementum, 23, 24

Chauliac, Guy de, 47

Cheeks, 28, 32

Chewing, 24, 25, 26, 27–28, 32, 34, 41, 50
Chew sticks, 70
Chlorhexidine, 67, 68
Computer Aided Design/Computer Aided
    Manufacturing (CAD/CAM), 93
Connective tissue fibers, 63
Copper, 46
Crown, 17, 23, 24, 37, 51, 53, 55, 57, 65,
    95, 99
    artificial, 50, 57, 93
    gold, 45, 50, 53
    infected, 40
    ivory, 53
    natural, 51
    porcelain, 50, 51
    post-and-core, 50
    tips, 17
Curettage, 67
Cuspids, 18, 19, 26. *See also* Canine teeth
Cusps, 26
Cutting bit, 14. *See also* Burs

Deciduous teeth. *See* Teeth: primary
Demineralization, 36
Dental arch, 32, 53, 58, 87
Dental checkups, 54
Dental college, 14, 15
Dental hygienist, 66, 70, 78
Dental prophylaxis, 78–79
Dental ridge, 32, 44, 53
Dental surgeons, 14
Dentifrices, 70, 74
Dentin, 23, 24, 36, 92, 98
Dentures, 14, 32, 44, 53, 93
Digestion, 25, 28
Disclosing agents, 77
Discoloring, 60
Drills, 14, 46, 48, 97, 99
    burs, 46
    high-speed water-cooled, 46, 49, 99
    low-speed, 46

Egyptians, 13, 52, 62
Elevator, 55

Enamel, 17, 23, 73, 78, 92, 95
Eruption, 17
Esophagus, 28
Ether, 47
Etruscans, 52
Evans, Thomas W., 47
Extractions, 45, 54
Eye teeth, 18. *See also* Cuspids

Face, 32, 40, 41, 83, 85
Facial reconstruction, 42
Fauchard, Pierre, 14
Fillings, 14, 46, 98
    amalgam, 46
    deep, 24
    porcelain, 46
    temporary, 55
Flossing, 37, 68, 70, 75, 77, 78, 79, 82, 99
Fluoridation, 73
Fluoride, 73, 75, 78, 92, 93
Full appliances, 83. *See also* Braces

Gingiva, 33, 37, 63, 68
    tissues, 34, 37. *See also* Gums
Gingivitis, 62, 65, 82
Gold, 51, 53
Gold foil, 46
Good Teeth (U.S. Public Health Service),
    71
Gram-negative aerobes, 62
Greeks, 14, 42, 66
Gregor, Don, 51
Gum disease, 55, 62, 63–65, 70, 75, 98.
    See also Periodontal disease
Gums, 19, 20, 23, 27, 33–34, 36, 37, 63,
    65, 66, 68, 75, 77, 82, 83, 95, 96, 99
    infected, 40, 53, 55, 62
    line, 71, 75, 77
    receding, 62, 95
    tissue, 57, 75, 95, 96

Hippocrates, 42
Hydrogen peroxide, 68
Hydroxyapatite, 44, 57

Implant therapy, 57–58
Impression tray, 50
Incisors, 19, 26, 30, 83
    central, 18
    lateral, 18
    lower, 18
    upper, 18

Jacket. *See* Crown: artificial
Jaffin, Robert A., 57, 58, 62, 63, 68
Jaw, 17, 19, 20, 24, 30, 33, 40, 41, 42, 51,
    53, 57, 85, 90
    alignment, 40, 87
    bone, 40, 53, 58, 61, 63, 79, 83, 85
    infection, 40, 53, 58
    injuries, 35
    joints, 82, 85
    lower, 32, 42, 44, 50, 58, 62, 83
    surgical removal of, 44
    upper, 32, 50, 83

Lasers, 92, 98, 99
Lips, 28, 32, 98

Malocclusion, 30, 82, 83
    surgical correction of, 88–90
    treatment of, 83–85, 90
Mandible, 32, 44, 90.
    See also Jaw: lower
Mastication muscles, 32
Maxilla, 32, 90. *See also* Jaw: upper
Maxillary arch, 32
Milk teeth, 17. *See also* Teeth: primary
Mineralization, 17
Mineral salts, 23
Mixed dentition, 19
Molars, 19, 20, 36, 78, 83
    first, 18, 29, 62, 65
    impacted, 39–40
    infected, 40
    and plaque, 36, 78
    second, 18, 26
    six-year, 18, 37
    third, 19, 20, 26, 27, 39

Mouth, 13, 17, 19, 23, 31, 32, 36, 41, 42,
    48, 57, 63, 65, 69, 70, 73, 85, 93, 95,
    99
Mouth rinse, 70, 71, 72, 75, 92
    fluoridated, 73, 74

National Institute of Dental Research
    (NIDR), 36, 40, 57, 62, 92, 98
National Institutes of Health, 36
Neck, 19, 23, 42
Nitrous oxide, 47. *See also* Anesthesia
Novocain, 48, 99. *See also* Anesthesia
Nutrition, 31, 99

Occlusal surface, 50. *See also* Chewing
Occlusion, 27, 32, 51
    line of, 32, 50
Open bite, 83
Opium poppy, 46
Oral cancer, 42
Oral epithelium, 17
Oral groove, 17
Oral irrigating devices, 68, 77
    electric, 77
    nonelectric, 77
Oral surgeon, 40, 42, 44, 90
Orthodontics, 81–90, 95
    appliances, 85–87, 95
    bands, 77, 87
    surgeons, 44, 57
    work, 23, 82
Orthodontic treatment, 85, 99
    cost of, 87–88
    interceptive, 85
Overbite, 83, 88

"Pearl," 23. *See also* Enamel
Penicillin, 39
Percoronitis, 40
Periodontal disease, 44, 57, 61, 62, 63, 67,
    68, 83, 91, 96, 97, 99. *See also* Gum
    disease
Periodontal ligament, 20, 21
Periodontal pockets, 63

Periodontists, 57, 96
Periodontitis, 63–65, 96
   localized juvenile (LJP), 63–64
Phoenicians, 52
Phosphorus, 17, 23, 79
Plaque, 36, 37, 46, 62, 63, 66, 67, 71, 75, 77, 78, 92
Pontics, 53. *See also* Teeth: replacement of
Premolars, 85
Prognathism, 83
Pronunciation, 29, 30
Prosthetics, 51, 53
Prosthodontics, 51, 93
Prosthodontists, 52
Public Health Service, U.S., 28, 71
Pulp, 17, 23, 24, 36, 37, 46
   chamber, 24, 55
   and decay, 53
   and gum disease, 53, 54
Pulpal nerves, 38
Pyorrhea, 63

Refined foods, 79–80
Remineralize, 78
Replantation, 58
Resorption, 40
Retaining appliance, 87
Romans, 13, 14, 42, 45, 46, 52, 66, 70
Root, 19, 20, 23, 33, 50, 53, 55, 63, 66, 87, 95
   planing, 65, 66
Root canal therapy, 50, 53–55

Saliva, 37, 48, 57, 65, 70, 73, 80
Saliva ejector, 48
Scaling, 14, 65, 68, 99
Scrapers, 14
Scraping, 70, 75
Siegeler, Howard, 42, 44
Silver, 46
Silver-palladium alloy, 51
Skeletal irregularities, 90
Sodium perborate, 68

Space retainer, 84, 85
Speech, 25, 28–31
"Spooning out." *See* Curettage
Starch, 36, 79
   refined, 80
Streptococcus mutans, 36
Stress, 65
Sugar, 23, 36, 80
   refined, 79
Surgeon Dentist: A Treatise on Teeth, The (Fauchard), 14

Tartar, 37, 62, 65, 67, 72, 73, 98. *See also* Calculus
Tartar-control products, 72
Teeth, 13, 14, 17, 40, 44, 49, 55, 69, 71, 72, 77, 79, 81, 85, 88, 90, 92, 98
   alignment, 19, 23, 29, 30, 82, 83, 87
   appearance, 81–82, 88, 99
   back, 62
   broken, 40
   buds, 17, 79
   cavities in, 38, 46, 48
   damaged, 50
   decay, 13, 36, 46, 50, 62, 70, 72, 73, 74, 75, 79, 95, 96, 97, 99
   devitalized, 50
   extraction of, 14, 45, 62
   fetal development of, 17
   formation of, 17–19
   fractures, 38, 40, 42
   function of, 25–31
   germs, 17
   impacted, 26, 27, 39, 55
   loss of, 32, 40
   lower, 18, 71
   nerveless, 50
   nerves in, 49
   permanent, 14, 15, 18, 19, 21, 32, 37, 78, 84, 85
   physical structure of, 15, 17–24
   polishing, 14, 79
   primary, 15, 17–19, 21, 26, 29, 84
   replacement of, 52, 53

restoration of, 45, 49, 50–60, 93, 96, 97
surfaces, 37
upper, 18, 71
Teething, 17, 18, 19
Temporomandibular joint, 32
Throat, 32
Thumb sucking, 83, 85
Tongue, 28, 29, 30, 69, 70, 85, 98
Toothache, 37, 53
Toothbrush, 36, 37, 71, 77
electric, 71
Toothbrushing, 37, 40, 69, 70, 77, 78, 82
Tooth fractures, 38, 40, 42
and infections, 39
Tooth gel, 71
Toothpastes, 71, 72, 73
fluoride, 73, 74, 78, 99
Tooth powder, 71, 72, 73
Tooth preparation, 50
Tooth reduction, 50
Tooth sealants, 78
Tooth worm, 46
Trauma, 40
and discoloration of teeth, 60
facial, 40

Trench mouth, 65, 68

Ultrasonics, 99

Vincent's Infection, 65.
See also Trench mouth
Vitamin A, 79
Vitamin C, 68, 79
Vitamin D, 79

Washington, George, 53, 70
Water
drinking, 73
fluoridated, 73, 74, 75, 78
Weak chin, 83
Wells, Horace, 47
Wisdom teeth, 19, 26, 39
extraction of, 40
impacted, 39, 40, 55
infected, 40.
See also Molars: third

X rays, 38, 40, 46, 54
stereoscopic, 41
Xylocaine, 48.
See also Anesthesia

Dorothy Siegel is a free-lance writer, specializing in health and medicine, education, and related subjects. A graduate of UCLA, she was a staff writer at *Good Housekeeping* magazine and has published eight books, three for young adult readers—including one about young people who have overcome serious handicaps. She lives in Fair Lawn, New Jersey.

Dale C. Garell, M.D., is medical director of California Children Services, Department of Health Services, County of Los Angeles. He is also associate dean for curriculum at the University of Southern California School of Medicine and clinical professor in the Department of Pediatrics & Family Medicine at the University of Southern California School of Medicine. From 1963 to 1974, he was medical director of the Division of Adolescent Medicine at Children's Hospital in Los Angeles. Dr. Garell has served as president of the Society for Adolescent Medicine, chairman of the youth committee of the American Academy of Pediatrics, and as a forum member of the White House Conference on Children (1970) and White House Conference on Youth (1971). He has also been a member of the editorial board of the *American Journal of Diseases of Children.*

C. Everett Koop, M.D., Sc.D., is former Surgeon General, deputy assistant secretary for health, and director of the Office of International Health of the U.S. Public Health Service. A pediatric surgeon with an international reputation, he was previously surgeon-in-chief of Children's Hospital of Philadelphia and professor of pediatric surgery and pediatrics at the University of Pennsylvania. Dr. Koop is the author of more than 175 articles and books on the practice of medicine. He has served as surgery editor of the *Journal of Clinical Pediatrics* and editor-in-chief of the *Journal of Pediatric Surgery.* Dr. Koop has received nine honorary degrees and numerous other awards, including the Denis Brown Gold Medal of the British Association of Paediatric Surgeons, the William E. Ladd Gold Medal of the American Academy of Pediatrics, and the Copernicus Medal of the Surgical Society of Poland. He is a chevalier of the French Legion of Honor and a member of the Royal College of Surgeons, London.

PICTURE CREDITS